HOW TO EXCEL

DURING CROSS-EXAMINATION

Techniques for Experts that Work

STEVEN BABITSKY, Esq.

JAMES J. MANGRAVITI, Jr., Esq.

S•E•A•K, Inc.
Legal and Medical Information Systems

Falmouth, Massachusetts

CONTENTS

Preface

Cross-examination is dreaded by most expert witnesses. It need not be. Most of the fear associated with cross-examination deals with the unknown. Questions such as What will he ask me?, How should I act?, Should I fight back?, and What if I get trapped? may race through an expert's mind. With proper preparation, cross-examination need not be formidable.

This book is designed to be a comprehensive yet easy-to-use guide for expert witnesses preparing for cross-examination. The authors have attempted to teach by example. Included are sample cross-examinations from leading experts and attorneys from across the United States. By following the techniques outlined throughout this book and by understanding the types of questions that may be asked, the expert witness should be well on his or her way to excelling during cross-examination.

Steven Babitsky, Esq.
James J. Mangraviti, Jr., Esq.

Acknowledgments

The authors wish to acknowledge the following persons whose assistance in the production of this book was invaluable: Ronald S. Beitman, Esq.; Steve Bernheim, BCFE, ACFE; John C. Cabaniss, Esq.; Paul R. Cox, Esq.; Christopher J. Day, Esq.; Jay W. Dankner, Esq.; David Goldstein, Esq.; William F. Kitzes, Esq.; Marc S. Klein, Esq.; Kenneth I. Kolpan, Esq.; Richard K. Latimer, Esq.; Kenneth M. Levine, Esq.; John M. Moscarino, Esq.; Joseph E. Scuro, Esq.; Geoff Shapiro, Esq.; and Yau Wu, PhD. The authors would also like to acknowledge the invaluable input of Dee Netzel, Kathy Lamson, Rebecca Monette, and Ellen Babitsky for their assistance in the production and editing of this book.

Related Products by SEAK, Inc.

<u>VIDEOS</u>

How to Perform an Excellent Independent Medical Evaluation (Order # OP939694)
>   To order or for more information call the AMA at: 1-800-621-8335.

How to be an Effective Medical Witness (Order # OP956994)
>   To order or for more information call the AMA at 1-800-621-8335.

How to Use The Guides to the Evaluation of Permanent Impairment (Five-video set)

>   1.   *The Musculoskeletal System,* by Robert H. Haralson, III
>   (Order # OP957794)
>   2.   *Impairment Evaluation, Records, and Reports,* by Joseph Sataloff, MD
>   (Order # OP95759)
>   3.   *The Respiratory System,* by Paul E. Epstein, MD
>   (Order # OP957794)
>   4.   *Pain,* by Christopher R. Brigham, MD
>   (Order # OP957894)
>   5.   *The Legal Perspective,* by Steven Babitsky, Esq.
>   (Order # OP957994)

<u>TEXTS</u>

The Independent Medical Evaluation Report: A Step-by-Step Guide With Models,
by Christopher R. Brigham, MD; Steven Babitsky, JD; and James J. Mangraviti, JD
>   (Order # OP916696)

<u>AUDIOTAPE PROGRAMS</u>

Achieving Success with Workers' Compensation
Achieving Success as a Medical Witness

<u>NEWSLETTERS</u>

Expert Witness Journal
Workers' Compensation Monthly
Occupational Medical Digest
Effective Medical Witness

To subscribe or for more information call SEAK at 508/548-7023. Inquiries may also be addressed to SEAK, Inc. at P.O. Box 729, Falmouth, MA 02541. Fax 508/540-8304; e-mail address: seakinc@aol.com; internet address: http://www.seak.com

About the Authors

Steven Babitsky, Esq., is a former trial lawyer who has represented thousands of injured workers and others with disabling conditions for over twenty years. He has been involved extensively in the arenas of workers' compensation, personal injury, and Social Security disability. He is a well-known author in this field and an experienced trainer. Attorney Babitsky serves as president of SEAK, Inc., a legal and medical information service organization. He also serves as editor of the *Expert Witness Journal* and as seminar leader for the annual Expert Witness and Litigation Seminar.

James J. Mangraviti, Jr., Esq., is also a former trial lawyer. He currently serves as vice-president of SEAK, Inc. He is a distinguished scholar and author. His publications include the texts *Understanding the AMA Guides in Workers' Compensation, Litigating Stress Cases in Workers' Compensation,* and *The Independent Medical Evaluation Report: A Step-by-Step Guide With Models.* Mr. Mangraviti is editor of the *Effective Medical Witness* newsletter.

Dedication

This text is dedicated to those expert witnesses who willingly put their reputations and credibility at risk each time they undergo cross-examination.

Chapter 1 The Effective Expert Witness

Overview

The Role of an Expert Witness

The role of an expert witness in the American judicial system is "to assist the trier of fact to understand the evidence, or to determine a fact in issue."[1] You qualify to be an expert witness through "knowledge, skill, experience, training, or education."[2] As an expert, you assist the trier of fact (i.e., the judge or jury) by rendering an opinion which will help prove or disprove a fact in issue. For example, a physician may be retained to render an opinion as to the level of impairment sustained by a plaintiff in a personal injury case.

Your role as an expert is to tell the truth and render an objective opinion. You will be a much more effective expert witness if you appear to be a "kindly teacher" and do not attempt to advocate for the party who has retained you.[3]

The attorneys in the case have a far different role. Although they are also obligated to tell the truth, they are ethically obligated to advocate the position of their respective clients. It is their job, not the expert's, to present the evidence to make it appear as favorable as possible to their clients.

Attorney Marc S. Klein describes the distinction between the roles of expert and attorney in the following way:

> The attorney is in court to act as an advocate, while the expert is not. As a trial lawyer, I have a duty to use my 'specialized knowledge' to convince others of my client's cause. As an expert, you have something else to contribute. You have a duty to honestly and objectively transmit your 'specialized knowledge' to the factfinder when the system depends on that knowledge for a rational result.[4]

The importance of expert witnesses in modern litigation cannot be overstated.

> In today's litigation, expert witnesses frequently determine the outcome of any given case. The influence they have on the outcome of any trial can never be overstated....

---

[1] Federal Rules of Evidence, Rule 702.
[2] Federal Rules of Evidence, Rule 702.
[3] Roberto Aron et al., *Cross-Examination of Witnesses: The Litigator's Puzzle* (1989) 331.
[4] Marc S. Klein, *How to Fight Back: The Rights and Remedies of Expert Witnesses* (Fifth Annual National Expert Witness and Litigation Seminar, June 1996) 77.

All good trial lawyers are well aware of this and know that many trials become nothing more than a battle of experts.[5]

Indeed, it has been found that litigants rely on expert testimony in approximately 80% of all civil cases and in one half of all felony prosecutions.[6]

Procedure for Testifying

The procedure for delivering your expert testimony is well known to experienced experts. We briefly review the applicable procedure for readers who have had less experience with the legal system.

When you have been retained as an expert witness, the attorney retaining you may call you to the witness stand to present evidence. He would do this through *direct examination*. Direct examination involves the attorney who called you as a witness, in this case the attorney who retained you as an expert, asking you a series of questions. Counsel carefully crafts these questions to elicit information that is favorable to his client. Frequently, retaining counsel will rehearse an expert's direct testimony prior to trial in a process known as "preparing the witness." When you have finished responding to direct examination, the other attorneys in the case will be allowed to question you through *cross-examination*. The attorney who retained you will then have another chance to question you in a process known as *redirect examination*.

How the Cross-Examining Attorney Prepares

In preparation for cross-examination, a good attorney will attempt to learn as much about you and your area of expertise as possible.[7] You should assume that he has a copy of everything you have ever had published, and may even have copies of your unpublished writings. The cross-examining attorney will often have a copy of your curriculum vitae and the transcripts of any testimony you have given in the past. You should also assume that the attorney has a good understanding of your area of specialty. He will obtain this knowledge by reviewing relevant literature and by being briefed by his own expert witnesses and consultants. Attorneys are paid to win. Do not underestimate the preparations they will undertake to increase their chances of success.

---

[5] C. D. Sullivan, "Expert Witnesses — Or Are They?," *Defense Counsel Journal* 58, no. 2 (Apr. 1991) 280.

[6] Marc S. Klein, "Why Judges and Juries Must Be Scientifically Literate," *NJL* 4 (Jan. 1995) 216.
[7] Roberto Aron et al., *Cross-Examination of Witnesses: The Litigator's Puzzle* (1989) 326.

Goals of the Cross-Examining Attorney

It is important to understand the goals of the attorney who is cross-examining you. She generally has three goals. The first is to lessen the impact of the testimony you gave on direct examination. This is done by discrediting you. The examining attorney can be expected to challenge your qualifications, intelligence, and bias. If counsel can succeed in destroying your credibility, the value of your direct testimony will be lost to the opposing side.

The second goal of the cross-examining attorney is to use you to support her client's position. This is done through questioning in which your opinion's underlying assumptions are varied. Counsel then seeks a new opinion which is favorable to her client.

The third goal of the cross-examining attorney is to directly attack your opinion. Skilled counsel will attempt to discredit the methodology by which you have arrived at your opinion. Counsel will also use extraneous sources such as learned treatises to contradict and discredit your opinion. She may also suggest to the jury that your opinion is simply absurd.

All of these goals reflect the mission of opposing attorneys. Their objective is to advocate their client's position. This is done by attempting to destroy the credibility of experts retained by other parties and by using those same experts to render opinions favorable to their clients.

Techniques Used by Counsel

It is helpful for you to understand, recognize, and be able to effectively deal with the techniques used to cross-examine expert witnesses. The eight fundamental techniques have been described eloquently by McElhaney:

1. Make the expert your witness; turn the testimony to support the opposite position.

2. Attack the field of expertise; show lack of recognition of the professional field.

3. Attack the witness' qualifications; establish gaps in the professional resume.

4. Expose the witness' bias; give reasons why testimony is partial.

5. Attack the witness' fact basis; prove investigation was inadequate.

6. Change the hypothetical used on direct; vary the facts to support the opposition if use of the hypothetical question is the basis for expert opinion.

7. Impeach the witness with learned treatises and journals; any authoritative, recognized text, can be used to cross-examine.

8. Attack the witness head-on.[8]

Ethical Violations by the Expert Witness

Counsel will frequently use cross-examination to uncover any ethical violations by the expert witness. Proof of an ethical violation can have a dramatic impact on the decision of the jury or fact finder. Common ethical violations by expert witnesses include:

- Outright false data
- Investigation not done
- Data altered
- Conditional engagement undertaken
- False testimony
- Intentional ignoring of available data
- Recanting prior contra positions
- Assignment beyond competence
- Accepting unauthorized attorney influence
- Inadequate support or time to complete assignment
- Conclusion reached before research
- Conflicts of interest[9]

Other ethical violations include *trimming* (smoothing irregularities to make data look accurate and precise), *cooking* (retaining only those results that fit the theory and discarding others), and *forging* (inventing research data).[10]

The Voice of Experience

What is it really like to be cross-examined by an experienced trial attorney? Here is how experienced expert witnesses describe the process:

> How does it feel to be boiled in your own blood? That is one of the many emotions I have felt during the cross-examination...the strategy is to impeach your testimony and destroy your credibility. They want to make you sound unbelievable to the jury.[11]

---

[8] McElhany, "Expert Witnesses," *ABA Journal* (Mar. 1989) 98-99.
[9] Harol A. Feder, *Shepard's Expert and Scientific Evidence Quarterly* 2, no. 4 (Spring 1995) 7-10.
[10] *Expert Witness Journal* (May 1995) 1.
[11] Jack V. Matson, *Effective Expert Witnessing* (Lewis Publications: 1990) 53.

The better you are as an expert and the better your reputation, the harder the opposing attorney will work to take you out and the better he will prepare for the battle.[12]

Being on the stand can be a psychologically numbing experience — faced with a relentless cross-examiner, questioning everything that you've said in court and often times out of court, can be traumatic.[13]

How do lawyers feel about cross-examining experts? Here is how two experienced trial attorneys describe how they approach cross-examination:

This may sound nasty, but you deserve to know that many trial attorneys (including me) take particular pleasure in knocking out dishonest or ignorant experts. I don't just mean from the case at hand. I mean ending their careers, with prejudice as we say.[14]

Cross-examination of an expert usually will resemble [the] peeling of an onion, exposing layer after layer of weaknesses, error and fallacy.[15]

General Advice

Maintain the Sympathy of the Jury

It is usually safe to assume that at the beginning of a cross-examination the jury will be sympathetic to you. This is a result of a number of factors, including the low level of esteem in which lawyers are currently held by society in general. To avoid losing the jury's sympathy you should be careful to not be arrogant, hostile, or unresponsive. You do not want to be perceived as a cocky hired gun.

It is very important to maintain the sympathy of the jury. In many cases jurors are unable to fully understand the expert testimony that is presented. They must therefore choose between two opinions which they do not fully understand. In these cases, jurors may base their decision on which expert presents himself better and seems more sympathetic to them. [16]

---

[12] Rigley, *Presenting Expert Testimony: Preparation and Delivery* (National Expert Witness and Litigation Seminar, June 1995).

[13] Dankner, *Preparing the Expert for Testimony and Trial* (SEAK, Inc., Fifth Annual National Expert Witness and Litigation Seminar, June 1996).

[14] Marc S. Klein, *How to Fight Back: The Rights and Remedies of Expert Witnesses* (SEAK, Inc., Fifth Annual National Expert Witness and Litigation Seminar, June 1996) 77.

[15] Michael E. Tigar, *Cross-Examination of Expert Witnesses* (1991) 224.

[16] Roberto Aron et al., *Cross-Examination of Witnesses: The Litigator's Puzzle* (1989) 327.

Stay Within Your Area of Expertise

You should not stray beyond your area of expertise. By restricting yourself to your own area of expertise you will help to establish and maintain your credibility. Consider the following example:

> **Q:** Mr. Smith, you previously testified that the airliner crash was caused by oxygen cylinders which ignited in the forward cargo hold, is that correct?
>
> **A:** Yes.
>
> **Q:** Was it a violation of established airline safety procedures to load filled oxygen cylinders onto a passenger jet?
>
> **A:** I can't answer that question, it is beyond my area of expertise.

> *Note:* The expert witness did not explain his answer and did not volunteer any other information. What he did was answer the question in a direct, succinct fashion.

Verbal Techniques

Always listen carefully to the question asked by counsel. Only answer the question asked. If counsel asks you, "Now, sir, do you have an opinion as to the cause of the collapse of the scaffolding which resulted in the injury to the plaintiff?," your answer must be "yes" or "no." Do not give a five-minute explanation of your opinion. Answer the question posed.

Make sure that you hear the question. A courtroom is a very stressful environment. If you are not absolutely sure that you heard the question correctly, ask that it be repeated.[17]

If you do not understand the question, say so. If you do not understand a term the attorney uses, or if the term has several meanings, have her define the term for you. Note, however, that these responses should never be given for the sole purpose of disrupting the cross-examiner.[18]

If you do not know the answer to a question say, "I don't know." Avoid answers such as "I don't have any specific knowledge," "I may have," "I have no direct evidence," "I don't think I did," "I probably had," and "I don't recall the details." Such answers will most likely be viewed by the jury as evasive and may result in a loss of credibility.[19] In addition, such answers invite additional cross-examination.

---

[17] William G. Mulligan, *Expert Witnesses: Direct and Cross-Examination* (1987) 8.
[18] William G. Mulligan, *Expert Witnesses: Direct and Cross-Examination* (1987) 8.
[19] Jack V. Matson, *Effective Expert Witnessing* (Lewis Publications: 1990) 52.

Q: How tall is the plaintiff?

A: I don't know.

Direct answers like the one above have the additional benefit of forcing counsel to move on. Additional questions on this point will be objected to as being asked and answered.

Many inexperienced expert witnesses have great difficulty in admitting that they do not know the answer to a particular question. Most attempts to hazard a guess end in disaster.

For example, here is an expert who should have replied that he did not know the education level of the decedent in a product liability case.

Q: Just so the record is clear. What was the educational level of Joseph Canty, do you know?

A: I doubt if he — I think he had elementary school education. I don't think he finished high school.

Q: You keep saying think, think. Do you know?

A: All I know is what was in the deposition, and I seem to recall that he did not have a high school degree.

Q: I am speaking now of Joseph Canty, the man who died.

A: Yes.

Q: He was illiterate, Doctor. Are you aware of that?

A: It's not stated as such.

Q: Maybe you are confusing Samuel Canty's deposition. What's the difference between Samuel Canty and Joseph Canty? Do you know who those two people are?

A: Are you trying to be condescending to me or patronizing to me?

Q: No, I am trying to get clear that we understand where we are going here. This is a serious matter.

A: There's no deposition of Joseph Canty.

Q: Because he died.

A: I know. Why did you say that?

Q: Because you keep referring to the deposition as though that's going to provide for the education level of Joseph Canty.

A: No. There's nothing in that that says that.

Q: So you don't know?

A: I don't know.

> **Q:** So you don't know....
>
> **A:** You asked me the question. I didn't say I knew the answer. I assumed that it wasn't a very good level of education, just based on my knowledge of sociology and demographics and things like that.

Limit your answer to what was asked

Do not go beyond what was asked. Volunteering information prolongs the cross-examination. It also can get you into trouble by moving you away from your proper role in the case, that of an expert witness, not an advocate.[20]

Counsel may cross-examine you with questions that are technically incorrect or are otherwise incomplete. Answer the question asked, not what you feel should have been asked. Even innocent violations of this cardinal rule can result in testimony that appears evasive. This can dramatically lessen your credibility. For example, consider this exchange:

> **Q:** Have you published any articles or books dealing with the subject of safety as regards ice hockey rinks?
>
> **A:** I'm preparing that standard. They alluded to that in the article that's been written by me.
>
> **Q:** My question is have you had any articles published?
>
> **A:** I'm in the process of doing that right now for a symposium.
>
> **Q:** Sir, my question is, have you prepared any articles that have been published dealing with safety relative to ice hockey rinks?
>
> **A:** It's been accepted for next springtime.
>
> **Q:** Has it been published?
>
> **A:** No, but I can show you a draft of the article that will be published in the springtime.

> *Note:* Not only has the expert failed to answer the simple question directly, he has volunteered information which could be used as further ammunition during cross-examination.

---

[20] William G. Mulligan, *Expert Witnesses: Direct and Cross-Examination* (1987) 8.

Do not argue with counsel

You can disagree, but never argue. For example, if counsel asks you if the chair collapsed due to poor construction, you should not respond that the weight of the plaintiff caused the collapse.

Be comfortable and be yourself

Find a style that fits and stick to it. Do not try to imitate the style of another expert. That style may work very well for the other expert, but might not be good for you.

Do not be arrogant or condescending

You want to appear sincere and credible. If you try to be flippant with the examining attorney you run the risk of offending the jury.[21] For example, you should not respond to a question on cross-examination with the response, "I'm not sure what you mean," when you understand the question. You should also be careful to be particularly polite and respectful to the judge, courtroom personnel, and the jury.

Think before you answer

Your testimony is being scrutinized by lawyers, a judge, and a jury. It is also being recorded verbatim by the court reporter. Take the time needed to form a carefully considered response.

Pause before giving your response

This will give your retaining attorney an opportunity to object if she so desires. It will also give you an opportunity to carefully consider your response.

---

[21] Roberto Aron et al., *Cross-Examination of Witnesses: The Litigator's Puzzle* (1989) 327.

Be an expert, not an advocate

Do not get involved in any of the lawyers' arguments or sidebar conferences.[22] When there is an objection, do not say anything else until you are instructed to do so by the judge.

Answer the questions directly

When an attorney asks an expert witness a question that can be answered directly, the failure to do so is generally a mistake. What often results is that the expert appears to be evasive and loses credibility. Thus, when the expert replies, "I don't have any specific knowledge," "I may have," "I have no direct evidence," "I don't think I did," "I probably had," and "I don't recall the details," he loses credibility with the jury.[23]

Here is an example of such an exchange:

Q: What is your consulting fee on this case?

A: My fee was between $120 and $150 per hour.

Q: Was it $120, $130, $140, or $150? Please be more specific.

A: As I stated, my fee was between $120 and $150 per hour.

Q: You mean that when you submitted an invoice you stated, "Pay me between $120 and $150 per hour"?

A: Ah, ah [stammers and stutters] I was paid between $120 and $150 per hour.[24]

Be formal during depositions

As an expert witness you may be deposed by counsel representing the opposing party. The informality of both the deposition setting and the attorneys can easily lull you into a false sense of security. Make no mistake, counsel is involved in a serious fact-finding mission in which your demeanor, expertise, and the manner with which your state your remarks will be scrutinized. These depositions are not the time to make jokes or to be lighthearted with counsel.

---

[22] Jack V. Matson, *Effective Expert Witnessing* (Lewis Publications: 1990) 61.

[23] Jack V. Matson, *Effective Expert Witnessing* (Lewis Publications: 1990) 68.

[24] Jack V. Matson, *Future of Expert Witnessing* (Seak, Inc., The Role of the Expert Witness in the 1990s and Beyond Seminar, April 1993).

Here is an example of a chemist who, due to the informal nature of counsel, made jokes and self-deprecating remarks during a product liability case which resulted in a death.

Q: Do you know who L. Barker is?

A: No. He used to play Tarzan, I think, but I am not sure.

Q: He could have.

A: He's one —

Q: He went on to be a great scholar in product labeling, but apparently you haven't read his work. Are you familiar with the very latest software product released by them called FPETTL 3.2?

A: No. Maybe 3.1, but not 3.2.

Q: Why don't you tell us the principles 3.1 operated on?

A: I was being facetious.

Q: Is there any way, as a scientist, that you have of determining whether that opened position, as well as the placement of the cans on top of the stove, occurred during the course of or subsequent to the fire or in fact prior to the fire?

A: Only by DNA testing. That's about the only way.

Q: Have you done such DNA testing?

A: I am kidding. I really — I think it's a tragic accident and all that, but of course there's no way to know.

Q: OK. I just have a few other questions to ask you, then we are done.

A: It's OK. I have half a can of soda to finish.

Q: These kind ladies and gentlemen may have additional questions.

A: Pick at the carcass.

Note: The expert witness probably felt that because his testimony was being taken by deposition this joking around was acceptable. In fact, however, by the end of the deposition there was little chance this expert would be called to testify in the case at hand or in any future cases.

Nonverbal Techniques

Dress appropriately. In most cases this means formal business attire. Make sure that you are well groomed and not wearing ostentatious jewelry. Do not chew gum. Remember that everything you do can be seen by the jury.

When walking in and out of the courtroom, do not look at or acknowledge the party who has retained you. Do not even stop to shake hands. If you do so, you will lose credibility with the jury. Furthermore, do not invade the space of the jury by leaning on the railing of the jury box.

While in the courtroom, try to appear calm and self-assured. Use good posture while sitting in the witness box. Be serious and professional. Have all your documents and notes organized so you do not have to fumble through them. If you like, practice by videotaping yourself giving mock testimony.

You can expect counsel to closely scrutinize your body language. Do not appear uncomfortable or insecure. Signs that you are insecure include frequently moving your hand to your mouth or face, fidgeting, toying with your clothes or hair, and finger or foot tapping.[25] These signs not only present a negative image to the jury, but an experienced attorney will also recognize them.

Documents Read Aloud

During cross-examination counsel may read from a document and ask you at the completion of the recitation, "Is that correct?" If you answer affirmatively, that answer can be construed as meaning not only that the attorney read the document correctly, but that you agree with the statement.

Here is a more effective way of handling that situation:

> **Q:** In Plaintiff's Exhibit No. 10 the statement contained says, "Your efforts at voluntary compliance are appreciated and if we can be of assistance please contact this office." Is that correct?
>
> **A:** That's what is written there.

> *Note:* The expert did not agree or disagree with the statement but merely acknowledged that it was read correctly. Remember to always carefully review the document before responding to questions about it.

Practice Testifying

A good way to master the verbal and nonverbal techniques of testifying during cross-examination is to practice. Schedule an appointment with your retaining attorney. Ask her to conduct a mock cross-examination of you in the privacy of her office. Ask her to question you with her most difficult questions. Then, listen to her feedback and improve

---

[25] Harold A. Feder, "Methods of Challenging Forensic Fraud and Unethical Behavior," *Shepard's Expert and Scientific Evidence Quarterly* 2, no. 4 (Spring 1995) 3.

your technique. You may also choose to have your practice testimony videotaped. You can then see how you will appear to the jury. Learning from the experience and mistakes of others is invaluable in becoming adept at dealing with cross-examination.

Prepare Thoroughly

To excel during cross-examination you must be thoroughly prepared. Robert F. Hanley concisely explains the value of thoughtful preparation:

> "Counsel, I have spent more time in court over the past twenty-five years than you have, so save your breath. Just put me on the stand and watch me fly."
>
> Thus spoke the expert witness. Sure, put him on the stand without preparation and watch your case fly out the window, along with his arrogance and incomprehensible testimony.
>
> Preparation is important for all witnesses. Preparation — hours and hours of preparation — is almost always essential for the expert witness.[26]

To prepare for cross-examination you must anticipate areas of weakness in your opinion. You should assume that counsel has retained his own expert in your field who will help him craft his cross-examination of you. If the theory on which you base your opinion is not universally accepted, be prepared to answer questions about that on cross-examination. If you did not personally verify the facts on which you based your opinion, be prepared to answer those questions as well. The more you can anticipate counsel's questions, the more you can be prepared for cross-examination. As noted above, counsel preparing you should assist with this task.

You will, however, need to do your homework and be prepared to list scholarly articles supporting your opinion. Review your curriculum vitae and be ready to answer questions about your qualifications.

Ask the counsel who has retained you what the other side's expert will say in opposition to you. This information can be obtained through a deposition transcript, interrogatories, or through a pre-trial memorandum. Prepare for cross-examination by anticipating questions that would support the other side's expert opinion.

You should help prepare your retaining attorney for trial.[27] Make sure that he thoroughly understands both your theory of the case and the theory of the opposing expert. Prepare your attorney for the weaknesses in your opinion that you expect to be highlighted during cross-examination. If your retaining attorney is to repair damage done

---

[26] Robert F. Hanley, "Preparing the Expert Witness" in *Expert Witnesses*, ed. Robert F. Rossi (ABA, 1991) 155.

[27] Douglas Danner and John W. Toothman, *Trial Practice Checklists* (1989) 287.

to you on cross-examination during his redirect examination, he must be properly prepared by you.

Protection by the Judge

The judge ultimately decides how far the cross-examining attorney is allowed to go when questioning you. Cross-examination is designed to be harsh. However, when an attorney crosses the line of appropriateness, the judge can step in to protect you from "harassment and undue embarrassment."[28] In making this determination, the trial judge will weigh "the importance of the testimony, the nature of the inquiry, its relevance to credibility, waste of time and confusion."[29]

Unfortunately, many judges have had mixed experiences with expert witnesses and are not sympathetic to their plight. Consider the following comment made by a federal judge:

> An expert can be found to testify to the truth of almost any factual theory, no matter how frivolous....At the trial itself, an expert's testimony can be used to obfuscate what would otherwise be a simple case....Juries and judges can be and sometimes are misled by such experts for hire."[30]

If you feel as though you are being abused, keep calm. Do not become arrogant or start to argue with the cross-examining attorney. If the cross-examiner is going too far, your retaining attorney will bring this to the judge's attention or the judge may take action without waiting for input from your retaining attorney. If you keep calm, the cross-examining attorney will be the one who loses credibility with the jury, not you.

---

[28] Federal Rules of Evidence, Rule 611(a).

[29] Advisory Committee Notes, Federal Rules of Evidence, Rule 611(a).

[30] Judge Jack B. Weinstein (United States District Court, Ninth Symposium on Statistics and the Environment, National Academy of Sciences, October 27, 1986).

Chapter 2 Qualifications and Methodology

Overview

Attorneys retain expert witnesses because of their qualifications, knowledge, ability to communicate, availability, and their ability to withstand cross-examination.

Under Federal Rule of Evidence 702, there are two distinct requirements for qualifying as an expert witness:

1. The witness must be qualified by knowledge, skill, experience, *or* education.

2. The expert's specialized knowledge must assist the trier of fact to understand the evidence or determine a fact in issue.[1]

Retaining counsel will qualify you on direct examination by asking you a series of questions intended to elicit your education, training, and experience. These questions will normally concern your:

- correct position, title, and duties
- education and degrees
- training
- current licenses
- areas of specialties and certifications
- membership in professional organizations and societies
- publications
- teaching activities
- professional accomplishments
- practical experience
- prior experience as an expert witness

At the conclusion of this preliminary questioning, opposing counsel may cross-examine you on your qualifications. The judge will then rule as to whether you qualify to testify.

In most cases, after the routine recitation of the expert's experience and training, she is found qualified. The direct examination and the cross-examination of the expert witness follows.

---

[1] Federal Rules of Evidence, Rule 702 provides if scientific, technical, or other specialized knowledge will assist the trier of fact to understand the evidence or to determine a fact in issue, a witness qualified as an expert by knowledge, skill, experience, training, or education, may testify thereto in the form of an opinion or otherwise.

Recently, the courts have started to increase the level of scrutiny given to the qualifications of expert witnesses. The following table lists recent cases in which expert witnesses were found not to be qualified or were otherwise prohibited from testifying. As the reader will note, this judicial scrutiny takes place with all types of expert witnesses.

Table 2-1: Experts Found Not Qualified or Testimony Rejected

Expert	Rejected Testimony	Citation
Actuary	Not permitted to testify that victim's gross earnings would triple in 17 years.	(NJ) *Williams v. Rene,* 72 F.3d 1096(3rd Cir. 1995)
Appraiser	Not permitted to testify about impact of prior engineering report.	(LA) *Nesbitt v. Dunn,* 672 So.2d 226 (La. App. 2 Cir. 1996)
Attorney	Not permitted to testify on fair trade practices of Robinson-Patman Act.	(WA) *Wlasiuk v. Whirlpool Corp.,* 914 P.2d 102 (Wash. App. Div. 1 1996)
Attorney	Not permitted to testify on ultimate issue in ADA case.	(CO) *Kuehl v. Wal-Mart Stores, Inc.,* 909 F.Supp. 794 (D.Colo. 1995)
Automotive Expert	Not permitted to testify on ultimate issue, i.e., lack of starter interlock system rendered car defective.	(MA) *Puopolo v. Honda Motor Co., Ltd.,* 668 N.E.2d 855 (Mass. App. Ct. 1996)
Cardiologist	Not permitted to testify on heart attack from nicotine patch.	(IL) *Rosen v. CIBA-Geigy Corp.,* 78 F.3d 316 (7th Cir. 1996)
CPA	Not qualified to testify on projected lost income.	(WV) *Maher v. Continental Cas. Co.,* 76 F.3d 535 (4th Cir. 1996)
Chemist	Testimony on cause of defective tire did not meet *Daubert* standard.	(LA) *Mitchell v. Uniroyal Goodrich Tire Co.,* 666 So.2d 727 (La.App.4 Cir. 1995)
Chiropractor	Not qualified to testify about TMJ.	(OH), *Fugett v. H,* 669 N.E.2d 6 (Oh. App. 2 Dist. 1995)
Civil Engineer	Not permitted to offer opinion on cause of escalator accident.	(NJ) *Jimenez v. GNOC Corp.,* 670 A.2d 24 (NJ Super. A.D. 1996)

Civil Engineer	Not qualified to testify about the standard of care of a general contractor.	(MO) *IMR Corp. v. Hemphill,* 926 S.W.2d 542 (Mo. App. E.D. 1996)
Clinical Psychologist	Opinion on custody rejected by trial judge.	(LA) *Warlick v. Warlick,* 661 So.2d 706 (La. App. 2 Cir. 1995)
Construction Expert	Not permitted to testify as to the cause and effect of delays.	(OH) *Jurgens Real Estate v. R.E.D. Constr.,* 659 N.E.2d 353(Ohio App.12 Dist. 1995)
Detective	Not permitted to speculate on rape suspect.	(NY*) Gomez By Gomez v. N.Y.C. Housing Authority,* 636 N.Y.S.2d 271 (A.D. 1 Dept. 1995)
Economics Professor	Not permitted to testify as to extent of investors' damages.	(NY) *Three Crown Ltd. Partnership v. Salomon Bros., Inc.,* 906 F.Supp. 876 (S.D.N.Y. 1995)
Economist	Not permitted to testify on enjoyment of life.	(NE) *Talle v. Nebraska Dept. of Social Serv.,* 541 N.W.2d 30 (Neb. 1995)
Economist	Not permitted to testify on value of enjoyment of life.	(NE) *Anderson v. Nebraska Dept. of Soc. Serv.,* 538 N.W.2d 732 (Neb. 1995)
Economist	Testimony on FELA injury inadmissible.	(VA) *CSX Transp. Inc. v. Casale,* 463 S.E.2d 445 (Va. 1995)
Emergency Room Physician	Not permitted to testify on head injury.	(TX) *Broders v. Heise,* 924 S.W.2d 148 (Tex. 1996)
Engineer	Not permitted to testify on defective tire.	(AZ) *Diviero v. Uniroyal Goodrich Tire Co.,* 919 F.Supp. 1353 (D.Ariz. 1996)
Engineer	Not permitted to testify on failure to mark curb.	(NY) *Guldy v. Pyramid Corp.,* 634 N.Y.S.2d 788 (A.D. 3 Dept. 1995)
Engineer	Not permitted under *Daubert* to testify on alternative design theory.	(IN) *Cummins v. Lyle Industries,* 93 F.3d 362 (7th Cir. 1996)
Engineer	Testimony of cause of spinout insufficient under *Daubert.*	(MI) *Pomella v. Regency Coach Lines Ltd.,* 899 F.Supp. 335 (E.D. Mich. 1995)
Ergonomics Expert	Not permitted under *Daubert* standard to testify on CAD design.	(TX) *Bennett v. PRC Public Sector, Inc.,* 931 F.Supp. 484 (S.D. Texas 1996)
Ergonomist	Not permitted to testify on keyboard design.	(NJ) *Dennis v. Pertec Computer Corp.,* 927 F.Supp. 156 (N.J. 1996)

Escalator Engineering Expert	Not permitted to testify on law.	(DC) *Weston v. Washington Metropolitan Area Transit*, 78 F.3d 682 (D.C. Cir. 1996)
Family Physician	Not qualified to testify on aplastic anemia.	(NY) *Corsetti v. Koopers Co., Inc.*, 640 N.Y.S.2d 556 (A.D. 1 Dept. 1996)
Friction Expert	Not permitted to testify on bathtub fall.	(NJ) *Fedorczyk v. Caribbean Cruise Lines, LTD*, 82 F.3d 69(3rd Cir. 1996)
Forensic Consulting Engineer	Not permitted to testify about effect of degreaser on parking lot.	(MO) *Scheerer v. Hardee's Food Systems, Inc.*, 92 F.3d 702 (8th Cir. 1996)
General Practitioner	Not qualified to testify on failed induced delivery.	(NH) *Chase v. Mary Hitchcock Memorial Hosp.*, 668 A.2d 50 (N.H. 1995)
Gastro-enterologist	Not qualified to testify about gynecological malpractice.	(OH) *Hudson v. Arias*, 667 N.E.2d 50 (Ohio App. 8 Dist. 1995)
Gynecologist	Not qualified to testify about blood recycling systems.	(ID) *Hollingsworth v. U.S.*, 928 F.Supp. 1023 (D. Idaho 1996)
Heroin Addict	Not qualified to testify on withdrawals.	(TX) *Pedraza v. Jones*, 71 F.3d 194 (5 Cir. 1995)
Horticulture Expert	Not permitted to testify about Benlate contamination.	(TX) *E.I. du Pont de Nemours & Co. v. Robinson*, 923 S.W.2d 549 (Tex. 1995)
Human Factors Psychologist	Not permitted to testify about unsafe gate.	(VA) *Chapman v. City of Virginia Beach*, 457 S.E.2d 798 (Va. 1996)
Investigating Officer	Not permitted to testify on cause of accident.	(GA) *McMichen v. Moattar*, 470 S.E.2d 800 (Ga. App. 1996)
Mechanical Engineer	Not permitted to testify on sudden acceleration of auto.	(LA) *Lawrence v. General Motors Corp.*, 73 F.3d 587 (5th Cir. 1996)
Metallurgy Engineer	Not permitted to testify about sewer grate.	(PA) *Colston v. Southeastern Pa. Transp.*, 679 A.2d 299 (Pa. Cmwlth. 1996)
Neurologist	Not permitted to testify about mental capacity based solely on the medical records.	(NY) *Tracy v. Steinberg*, 634 N.Y.S.2d 198 (A.D. 2 Dept. 1995)
Neurosurgeon	Testimony insufficient under *Daubert* on carpal tunnel syndrome.	(IL) *Dukes v. Illinois Cent. R. Co.*, 934 F.Supp. 939 (N.D. Ill. 1996)

Nuclear Reactor Physicist	Testimony on TMI insufficient under *Daubert* standard.	(PA) *In Re TMI Litigation Cases Consolidated II,* 911 F.Supp. 775 (M.D. Pa. 1996)
Nurse	Not qualified to testify in medical malpractice claim.	(PA) *Flanagan v. Labe,* 666 A.2d 333 (Pa. Super. 1995)
Occupational Physician	Not permitted to testify on state-of-the-art of asbestos hazards.	(OH) *Owens-Corning Fiberglas v. A.M. Centennial,* 660 N.E.2d 819 (Ohio Com. Pl. 1995)
Ophthal-mologist	Not permitted to testify as to chemical cause of cataracts.	(NH) *Grimes v. Hoffman-LaRoche, Inc.,* 907 F.Supp. 33 (D.N.H. 1995)
Orthopedic Surgeon	Not permitted to testify on effect of litigation.	(MO) *Yingling v. Hartwig,* 925 S.W.2d 952 (Mo. App. W.D. 1996)
Orthopedic Surgeon	Not qualified to testify as to chiropractic malpractice.	(IA) *Brodersen v. Sioux Valley Memorial Hosp.,* 902 F.Supp. 931 (N.D. Iowa 1995)
Pathologist	Not qualified to testify on standard of care of surgeon.	(NY) *Good v. Presbyterian Hosp. in City of New York,* 934 F.Supp. 107 (S.D.N.Y. 1996)
Police Officer	Not permitted to testify about why motorist was negligent and why negligence caused accident.	(SD) *Robbins v. Buntrock,* 550 N.W.2d 422 (S.D. 1996)
Physician	Not permitted to testify on effects of CCP.	(NJ) *Rutigliano v. Valley Business Forms,* 929 F.Supp. 779 (D. N.J. 1996)
Physician	Not qualified to testify on polythermia.	(IL) *Muzzey v. Kerr-McGee Chemical Corp.,* 921 F.Supp. 511 (N.D. Ill. 1996)
Physician	Not permitted to testify that TCE caused birth defects.	(PA) *McKenzie v. Westinghouse Elec. Corp.,* 674 A.2d 1167 (Pa. Cmwlth. 1996)
Physician	Testimony insufficient to prove polysporin spray caused frostbite.	(TX) *Burroughs Wellcome Co. v. Crye,* 907 S.W.2d 497 (Tex. 1995)
Planning Regulator	Not qualified to testify on value of landowner's development rights.	(NV) *Suitum v. Tahoe Regional Planning Agency,* 80 F.3d 359 (9th Cir. 1996)
Podiatrist	Not permitted to testify on defect in basketball shoe.	(IN) *Tucker v. Nike, Inc.,* 919 F. Supp. 1192 (N.D. Inc. 1995)

Police Officer	Not permitted to testify as to the cause of an accident.	(OR) *Madrid v. Robinson*, 906 P.2d 855 (Or. App. 1995)
Political Activist	Not permitted to testify on health risks of EMF.	(GA) *Banks v. Georgia Power Co.*, 469 S.E.2d 218 (Ga. App. 1996)
Professor of Securities Law	Not permitted to testify about statements not actionable under securities law.	(NY) *Ausa Life Ins. Co. v. Dwyer*, 899 F.Supp. 1200 (S.D.N.Y. 1995)
Psychologist	Not qualified to testify as to sexual predator.	(WA) *In Re Twining*, 894 P.2d 1331 (Wash.App. Div. 3 1995)
Professor of Biochemistry	Not permitted to testify on testing of lung tissue.	(IL) *Braun v. Lorillard, Inc.*, 84 F.3d 230 (7th Cir. 1996)
Professor of Criminology	Not permitted to testify about deadly force.	(LA) *Hattori v. Peairs*, 662 So.2d 509 (La.App. 1 Cir. 1995)
Psychology Professor	Not permitted to testify about truthfulness.	(IA) *In Interest of S.J.M.*, 539 N.W.2d 496 (Iowa App. 1995)
Psychologist	Not permitted to testify as to credibility.	(NE) *Westcott v. Crinklaw*, 68 F.3d 1073 (8th Cir. 1995)
Pulmonologist	Not qualified to testify as to occupational asthma.	(NJ) *Diaz v. Johnson Matthey, Inc.*, 893 F.Supp. 358 (D.N.J. 1995)
Quarter Horse Expert	Not qualified to testify about partially blind horse.	(IN) *Ansick v. Hillenbrand Industries, Inc.*, 933 F.Supp. 773 (S.D. In. 1996)
Radiation Expert	Not permitted to testify in Three Mile Island case.	(PA) *In Re TMI Litigation Cases Consolidated II*, 910 F.Supp. 200 (M.D. Pa. 1996)
Roofing Expert	Not permitted to testify about negligence.	(SD) *Zens v. Hon*, 538 N.W.2d 794 (S.D. 1995)
Sexual Harassment Expert	Not permitted to testify that plaintiff was a victim of sexual harassment.	(ID) *Fowler v. Kootenai County*, 918 P.2d 1185 (Idaho 1996)
Sports Experts	Not qualified to testify on danger recognition.	(NE) *McIntosh v. Omaha Public Schools*, 544 N.W.2d 502 (Neb. 1996)
State Trooper	Not qualified to testify as to standard of care.	(PA) *Christiansen v. Silfies*, 667 A.2d 396 (Pa. Super. 1995)
Surgeon	Not permitted to rely on discussions with doctors on national standard of care.	(DC) *Travers v. District of Columbia*, 672 A.2d 566 (D.C. App. 1996)

Traffic Control Devices	Expert not qualified to testify about portable speed bumps.	(FL) *Goodyear Tire & Rubber Co., Inc. v. Ross,* 660 So.2d 1109 (Fla. App.4 Dist. 1995)
Trainmen	Not permitted to testify on engine cab design.	(KY) *Rice v. Cincinnati, New Orleans & Pacific Ry. Co.,* 920 F.Supp. 732 (E.D. Ky. 1996)
Transportation Consulting Engineer	Not permitted to testify as to who was driving vehicle in question.	(FL) *State Farm Mut. Auto. Ins. Co. v. Penland,* 668 So.2d 200 (Fla. App. 4 Dist. 1995)
Title Abstractor	Not qualified to testify on land ownership.	(UT) *Butler Crockett v. Pinecrest Pipeline,* 909 P.2d 225 (Utah 1995)
Tire Designer	Not permitted to testify on defective tire.	(AL) *Charmichael v. Samyang Tires, Inc.,* 923 F.Supp. 1514 (S.D. Ala. 1996)

The *Daubert* Challenge

In complex, novel, or substantial cases, opposing counsel may attempt to block completely or limit the scope of the expert witness testimony by the filing of a motion in limine. The basis of this motion frequently is a *Daubert* challenge.

During a *Daubert* challenge to your opinion the judge must decide whether the underlying reasoning of your opinion is scientifically valid and can be properly applied to the facts at issue. To make this decision, the judge will conduct a *Daubert* hearing. During the *Daubert* hearing you may be called upon to testify outside of the presence of the jury. In making his decision, the judge will consider many factors, including:

- Has the theory or technique in question been tested?
- Has it been subjected to peer review and publication?
- Is there a known or potential error rate?
- Is there widespread acceptance of the theory or technique within the relevant scientific community?

You should be prepared to answer all of these questions during a *Daubert* hearing. If your answers are insufficient, the judge may find that your underlying reasoning is insufficient and use the *Daubert* case to preclude you from testifying in front of the jury. Alternatively, the judge could limit the scope of the testimony you will be permitted to give.

The Federal Judicial Center's *Reference Manual on Scientific Evidence* states the following with regard to *Daubert* motions in limine and expert witnesses:

> Objections to evidence raised before trial are best presented by a motion in limine under Federal Rule of Evidence 104(a). In its recent decision in *Daubert*, the Supreme Court stated:

> Faced with a proffer of expert scientific testimony, then, the trial judge must determine at the outset, pursuant to Rule 104(a), whether the expert is proposing to testify to (1) scientific knowledge that (2) will assist the trier of fact to understand or determine a fact in issue.

> Rule 104(a) is the court's vehicle for determination of preliminary questions concerning the qualifications of a witness, the existence of a privilege, or the admissibility of evidence. The court may, if necessary, conduct a hearing (which must be outside the hearing of the jury), and it is not bound by the rules of evidence. When the admissibility of expert evidence is pivotal to a motion for summary judgment, a Rule 104(a) hearing should precede consideration of the motion. A ruling on admissibility may also be important in jurisdictions where the court may be precluded from granting judgment as a matter of law after trial on the ground that it had erroneously admitted expert testimony.

> By requiring the parties to follow the disclosure procedure under Federal Rule of Civil Procedure 26(a)(2), the court will have before it the complete statement of the opinions to which the expert will testify and their factual basis. This material, supplemented by memoranda addressed to the evidentiary issues, will provide a helpful record for rulings under Rule 104(a).[2]

Under *Daubert,* the judge will seek to determine if the expert's proposed opinion is supported by scientific reasoning and methodology. Thus, to survive a *Daubert* challenge in a motion in limine, the expert witness must use an appropriate methodology to ensure that her opinion derives from and constitutes a form of specialized knowledge.

All experts should be aware that judges undertaking a *Daubert* analysis will scrutinize their credentials, investigation, methodology, and conclusions very closely. Experts unprepared for such intense scrutiny should think carefully before accepting an engagement in this type of situation.

For example, when a neurosurgeon attempted to testify in a Federal Employer's Liability Act (FELA) case that an employee developed carpal tunnel syndrome (CTS), the physician was cross-examined closely about studies and investigations he performed in reaching his conclusions.

> **Q:** So with regard to carrying railroad signal lights, you have no empirical evidence from either studying it yourself or someone else studying it, the number of minutes or hours a day Mr. Dukes carried signal lights?

---

[2] Federal Judicial Center, *Reference Manual on Scientific Evidence* (1994) 30.

A: Only Mr. Dukes would know that, and that's by going from his memory. Perhaps his supervisors might know.

Q: So what you are saying is there really is no way to determine at what point Mr. Dukes can be employed as a train car inspector and carry these signal lights and not have any greater risk of developing carpal tunnel syndrome than the general population?

A: I agree to that. It is difficult to say at what point.

The doctor was unable to point to any scientific or objective sources to demonstrate the reliability of his opinions. According to the judge, the physician's opinions were based not on a factual or scientific basis, but merely on his own subjective observations.

The cross-examination of the expert continued to focus on the lack of objective studies or scientific evidence of causation.

Q: Doctor, what medical evidence do you have in the form of objective diagnostic studies that would demonstrate that there was a marked change...in the orthopedic pathology in his wrist from the date he started carrying these signal lights until the time he developed carpal tunnel syndrome?

A: The evidence is based on a clinical impression, not objective scientific data. It is based on my understanding of Mr. Dukes, his occupation, and the carpal tunnel syndrome.

Q: Do you have any empirical, medical, or scientific evidence that would support the conclusion that the carrying of signal lights accelerated his carpal tunnel syndrome condition?

A: It's a clinical opinion. It's not empirical, scientific evidence, as we've gone through. So the answer is no.

Q: Are you aware of any studies prior to 1991, when Mr. Dukes first presented with carpal tunnel syndrome symptoms regarding the carrying of objects such as signal lights and safe doses or exposures? Or, make it a compound question: doses or exposures beyond which the risk of developing carpal tunnel syndrome is increased?

A: My answer again is I cannot cite you a reference as I sit here today, but Illinois Central Railroad would have access to all the medical information about carpal tunnel syndrome which indirectly would implicate such activities in causing it.

Q: Doctor, are you aware of a strong statistical correlation between the activities engaged in by Mr. Dukes as a car inspector and the occurrence or incidence of carpal tunnel syndrome?

A: If you are asking me about precise statistics, I would have to say no, but what I have been asked to make is a clinical judgment about what contributed to his condition of carpal tunnel syndrome.

The expert was then cross-examined on his inability to identify any studies regarding the effects of carrying street lights:

Q: Have you ever been out to the railroad to observe what a car inspector does?

A: I have ridden on trains and seen people inspecting cars.

Q: Again, Doctor —

A: You mean was I specifically asked by Goldbert, Weisman, & Cairo to go out to Illinois Central Railroad to see what a car inspector does? No.

Q: Or any other freight carrier railroad. Have you gone out to any other railroad to observe what a car inspector does in his day-to-day tasks as a car inspector?

A: No.

Q: Have you interviewed any railroad personnel regarding their personal experiences with the carrying of signal lights?

A: No.

Q: Do you know if the handle is on the top, the left side, the right side, the bottom, the back, the front? Do you know where the handle is?

A: Not exactly.

Q: Do you know how these lights are balanced when they are held by the handle?

A: No.

Q: Do you know if Mr. Dukes was carrying these lights in the manner in which they were designed to be carried?

A: I guess that would be an assumption, so I would say no.

Q: Doctor, have you, for purposes of this case or any other carpal tunnel matter that you have reviewed, conducted any personal scientific research on the carrying of signal lights and carpal tunnel syndrome?

A: I believe I already answered that, and the answer is no.

Q: What about scientific studies with carrying and the development of arthritic wrists — have you done any personal research or scientific research or studies with regard to carrying any sort of object and the development of arthritic wrists?

A: No.

Note: As mentioned previously, this level of scrutiny of the expert witness and his methodology normally arises only in complex, novel, or substantial cases. If involved in such a case, it is crucial to make sure that you are qualified to serve as an expert on the particular issue in dispute. When you decline a case because you feel you are not qualified, you do a service to yourself and to your reputation and credibility. You also do a service to the attorney who sought to retain you.

As Table 2-2 illustrates, the extent to which *Daubert* has influenced expert witness testimony is evident in the recent cases in which expert witnesses were not permitted to testify due to failure to meet the *Daubert* standard.

Table 2-2: Testimony Excluded Under *Daubert*

Expert	Citation
Accident Reconstructionist	*Buckman v. Bombardier Corp.,* 893 F.Supp. 547 (E.D. N.C. 1995)
Biologist	*In Re Hanford Nuclear Reservation Litigation,* 894 F. Suppp. 1436 (E.D. Wash. 1995)
Cardiologist	*Rosen v. CIBA-Geigy Corp.,* 78 F.3d 316 (7th Cir. 1996)
Cardiologist	*Rosen v. CIBA-Geigy Corp.,* 892 F.3d 208 (N.D. Ill. 1995)
Chemist	*Mitchell v. Uniroyal Goodrich Tire Co.,* 666 So.2d 727 (La. App. 4 Cir. 1995)
Economist	*Dennis v. Pertel Computer Corp.,* 927 F.Supp. 156 (D.N.J. 1996)
Economist	*In Re Aluminum Phosphide Antitrust Litigation,* 893 F.Supp. 1497 (D.Kan. 1995)
Engineer	*Cummins v. Lyle Industries,* 93 F.3rd 362 (7th Cir. 1996)
Engineer	*Divieno v. Uniroyal Goodrich Tire Co.,* 919 F.Supp. 1353 (D.Ariz. 1996)
Engineer	*Officer v. Teledyne Republic Sprague,* 870 F.Supp. 408 (D.Mass. 1994)
Ergonomics Expert	*Bennet v. PRC Public Sector Inc.,* 931 F.Supp. 484 (S.D. Tex. 1996)
Failure Analysis Expert	*Cook v. American S.S. Co.,* 53 F.3d 733 (6th Cir. 1995)
Helicopter Mechanic	*Frosty v. Textron Inc.,* 891 F.Supp. 551 (D.Or. 1995)
Mechanical Engineer	*Pestel v. Vermeer Mfg. Co.,* 64 F.3d 382 (8th Cir. 1995)
Neurosurgeon	*Dukes v. Illinois Cert. R. Co.,* 934 F.Supp. 939 (N.D. Ill. 1996)

Physician	*Rutigliano v. Valley Business Forms,* 929 F.Supp. 779 (D.N.J. 1996)
Physician	*Summers v. Missouri Pacific R.R. System,* 897 F.Sup. 533 (E.D. Okl. 1995)
Physician	*Whiting v. Boston Edison Co.,* 891 F.Supp. 12 (Mass. 1995)
Podiatrist	*Tucker v. Nike Inc.,* 919 F.Supp. 1192 (N.D. Ind. 1995)
Professor of Biochemistry	*Braun v. Lorillard Inc.,* 84 F.3d 230 (7th Cir. 1996)
Psychologist	*Gier v. Educational Service Unit No. 16,* 845 F.Supp. 1342 (D.Neb. 1994)
Psychologist	*Gier by and Through Gier v. Educational Ser. Unit,* 66 F.3d 940 (8th Cir. 1995)
Tire Designer	*Carmichael v. Samyang Tires Inc.,* 923 F.Supp. 1514 (S.D. Ala 1996)
Toxicologist	*Cavallo v. Star Enterprises,* 892 F.Supp. 756 (E.D. Va. 1995)

An Assault on Your "Expertness"

Even if you are found by the judge to be qualified to testify, counsel will attempt to challenge and diminish your standing to render an expert opinion. This is done to lessen the weight your testimony is to be given by the fact finder. It may also be done to contrast your qualifications with those of an expert retained by the opposing party. The jury's assessment of the expert's qualifications often influences the weight given to an expert's opinion.[3]

An expert witness is qualified through "knowledge, skill, experience, training, or education."[4] All of these areas are fair game on cross-examination. If your qualifications are less than stellar, you can expect to be questioned about them on cross-examination. On the other hand, if you have very strong qualifications, you may not be questioned on them at all on cross-examination. A skillful attorney realizes that any questioning regarding strong qualifications only serves to reinforce your credibility, not destroy it.[5]

---

[3] Robert L. Habush, *Art of Advocacy: Cross-Examination of Non-Medical Experts* (1989) 4-3.
[4] Federal Rules of Evidence, Rule 702.
[5] Robert L. Habush, *Art of Advocacy: Cross-Examination of Non-Medical Experts* (1989) 4-4.

Provide an Accurate Curriculum Vitae

You can assume that counsel will have a copy of your latest as well as prior versions of your curriculum vitae (CV). It is extremely important that your CV contains no exaggerations or inaccuracies. If you did not graduate from MIT, summa cum laude, your CV should not indicate that you did. The date that you received a degree can also be used in cross-examination. If you list yourself as an author of a book or article and you were in fact only a co-author, you are opening yourself up to be damaged during cross-examination. If counsel can show that you exaggerated your CV, he can make the argument that you are exaggerating when giving your opinion. Even worse, if there is an obvious falsehood on your CV, counsel can portray you as a liar.

Licensing

You can expect counsel, in preparation for cross-examination, to investigate your background. He will contact the licensing agency of any professional license you hold to verify that you hold that license in good standing and to determine any disciplinary history. You can also expect that computer searches have been performed to verify what you have written (and also to use your writings to impeach you). Finally, counsel will also try to expose subtleties in your CV, such as the fact that the company you are president of is merely a one man-consulting firm.[6]

Gaps in Your Curriculum Vitae

A good attorney will cross-examine you in reference to any gaps in your curriculum vitae. You and your retaining counsel should be prepared to respond accordingly. The following exchange is a cross-examiner's ideal situation. It contains the types of devastating admissions which can destroy your credibility. While not all gaps in a CV are so blatant, even subtle ones will be utilized by diligent counsel. If you have a questionable area as does the doctor in this case, you should have a very good explanation that your retaining attorney can bring out either during direct examination or on redirect examination.

> **Q:** Sir, I have your curriculum vitae here. There is no indication where you were employed from July of 1992 through March of 1993. Is that correct?
>
> **A:** Yes, it is.
>
> **Q:** Were you employed during that period?
>
> **A:** No.
>
> **Q:** Were you looking for a job during that time?

---

[6] Robert L. Habush, *Art of Advocacy: Cross-Examination of Non-Medical Experts* (1989) 4-4.

A: Yes, I was.

Q: And why did you leave your previous employment?

A: I was terminated.

Q: Involuntarily?

A: Yes.

Q: When you say terminated involuntarily, you mean fired, do you not?

A: I was terminated.

Q: Isn't it a fact, sir, that you were terminated for repeated failure to follow hospital procedure?

A: That's what the hospital claimed, yes.

Knowledge, Skill, Experience, Training, and Education

You can anticipate that counsel will try to minimize and devalue your qualifications as an expert witness. That is, she will attempt to highlight weaknesses in your knowledge, skills, experience, training, and education. Expect close questioning in these areas.

Education

You can expect counsel to first and foremost highlight any obvious weak areas in your educational background. For example:

> **Q:** Sir, you received an AA degree from a two-year community college, is that correct?
>
> **Q:** It took you three and a half years to complete that degree, correct?
>
> **Q:** You next attended a series of three universities before completing your BA degree?
>
> **Q:** It then took you three years to complete your BA?
>
> **Q:** And the BA you were finally awarded was in communications?
>
> **Q:** You were never awarded any advanced degrees such as a masters or a PhD, is that correct?
>
> **Q:** In fact, your grade point average at the three universities was a 2.1, was it not?
>
> **Q:** Isn't it a fact that you need at least a 2.0 to graduate?
>
> **Q:** You just made it, didn't you sir?

The best way to deal with questions of this type is to answer them directly. If the answer is affirmative, simply admit it and wait for the next question. If you try to be evasive or defensive this will only highlight the holes in your education and make them seem more significant.

As an expert witness, if you exaggerate or lie about your academic accomplishments in your CV or in your answers to interrogatories, depositions, or at trial, you will be subject to intensive cross-examination. The impact on the jury or fact finder will be twofold. First, they will learn that you lied or exaggerated and thus cannot be believed. Second, they will learn of your failures in excruciating detail and may eventually suspect your qualifications.

Here is an example of the cross-examination of an engineer when he exaggerated his academic accomplishments:

Q: OK. Now, going back to your earlier work, you did well in your classes at Mississippi State, is that correct?

A: I don't know exactly the grade point average.

Q: Did you tell us at deposition that you did well?

A: Yes.

Q: And did you do well in your classes at the University of Missouri, Columbia?

A: I don't know the grade point average. In other words, I don't know what the grades were. That's over 30 years ago.

Q: Are these all the colleges that you went to?

A: There was a summer class. I took a single class in Memphis, Tennessee, while I was working there during the summer.

Q: OK. What school was that?

A: Christian Brothers College.

Q: And you just took one course there?

A: I took a summer class there, yes.

Q: OK.

Judge, may I approach the witness?

      THE COURT: Yes sir.

Q: I'm handing you Plaintiff's Exhibit 225. Could you tell the jury what it is?

A: That appears to be a transcript of my grades.

Q: First of all, grades are typically confidential with a school, aren't they?

A: Yes.

Q: Have you ever released those publicly?

A: No, I haven't.

Q: So you have no idea how I would have gotten those grades.

A: No, I wouldn't.

Q: OK. Sir, I'm going to hand you now what is Plaintiff's Exhibit 226, which I'll represent to you is a certified copy of your application to become a professional engineer. And I'll ask you, sir, if your grades are attached to that information.

A: Yes, it looks like they are.

Q: So, having had the benefit of looking at that, do you now recall that you, in fact, submitted those to the Texas licensing board?

A: Yes, I did.

Q: Now, directing your attention to the classes that you took, and in particular your work at the University of Missouri, Columbia, in the first term, isn't it true that you flunked college algebra?

A: Yes, I did.

Q: And you got a D in trigonometry?

A: Yes.

Q: And you got a D in American history?

A: Yes.

Q: And then you were placed on probation?

A: That's correct.

Q: And second semester, as well, indicates you were on probation?

A: Yes. I had C's during the semester.

Q: And then in the summer you took the one course at Christian Brothers College, isn't that correct?

A: Yes, the one I got a B in.

Q: Correct. In economics. Then you went back to the University of Missouri, Columbia, for the first semester in 1964/65. Isn't it true that you flunked calculus?

A: Yes.

Q: And doesn't it indicate you were dismissed from school?

A: That's correct.

Q: And then in the second semester of 1964/65, you took a math analysis course at Christian Brothers College, didn't you?

A: Yes, I did.

Q: And you withdrew from that class in March of '65, didn't you?

A: No. You'll notice it says "audit."

Q: Down below — I'm sorry. Go ahead.

A: It says "audited." That was a class I audited until I went into the Air Force. I withdrew at the point where I went into the Air Force.

Q: And then did you go back, sir, second semester of 1965/66 to Christian Brothers College in Memphis?

A: I'm sorry, I lost you. Where are you?

Q: Bottom of the left-hand column there, second semester, 1964/65.

A: OK.

Q: You went back to Christian Brothers College in Memphis, isn't that true?

A: Yes.

Q: And you withdrew from two of the classes you were taking that term, did you not?

A: That's right. I withdrew passing.

Q: Then in the fall of 1966/67 you went to Mississippi State; correct?

A: Yes.

Q: And you flunked calculus that first term?

A: That's correct.

Q: And you got a D in general physics?

A: Right.

Q: And then you got your first A in school that term, did you not —

A: Physical education.

Q: — in college. In bowling?

A: Yes.

Q: And spring semester 1966/67, you got your second A in college, and that was in principles of insurance?

A: Yes.

Q: But the same semester you flunked the computer course you were taking?

A: I'm sorry?

Q: You flunked the course called IE 423, digital comp. fundamentals?

A: Yes. Yeah, that was a period of time when I found out my father had cancer.

Q: And you flunked that computer course?

A: Yes.

Q: And you flunked calculus?

A: Yes.

Q: And you got a D in physics?

A: Yes. That was a bad time.

Q: And you got a D in European literature?

A: Yes.

Note: Retaining counsel proceeded during redirect examination to attempt to rehabilitate his expert by pointing out that Einstein and Edison had problems in school as well. It is clear that this expert was neither Einstein nor Edison. The witness was caught in a lie about his grades because counsel was able to obtain a copy of his transcripts. Experts should always assume that counsel will obtain all documents that can be damaging to their credibility.

Professional writings

You can also expect to be questioned about your professional writings. Counsel will attempt to emphasize that your writings are limited or have no relevance to the particular area on which you have been called to render an opinion. Counsel will attempt to suggest that this brings your qualifications in the case at hand into question.

> **Q:** Now, Mr. Jones, in the last thirty years you have published seventy articles in professional journals, have you not?
>
> **A:** That is correct.
>
> **Q:** As a matter of fact, all of these articles were published on semiconductor design, weren't they?
>
> **A:** Yes, they were.
>
> **Q:** This case is not about semiconductor design, is it?
>
> **A:** No, it is not.

> *Note:* In this situation the expert will usually attempt to explain that the principles involved are the same or similar.

Counsel may also attempt to show that you have written articles in areas in which you have limited training and are not truly an expert. The inference that counsel would like the jury to draw is that if you write on topics on which you are not an expert, you may also testify on topics on which you are not an expert.[7] See the following example:

> **Q:** Another article you wrote was about boating safety?
>
> **A:** That's correct.
>
> **Q:** Are you an expert in boating safety?
>
> **A:** I wouldn't consider myself an expert, no.
>
> **Q:** You're not a marine engineer, are you?
>
> **A:** No, I am not.

---

[7] Robert L. Habush, *Art of Advocacy: Cross-Examination of Non-Medical Experts* (1989) 4-43.

Q: You're not a ship pilot or anything like that, are you?

A: No.

Q: And you don't have any affiliation with the Coast Guard?

A: No.

Q: Or the Navy?

A: No.

Q: But you wrote this article on boating safety?

A: That's correct.[8]

Fellowships and grants

You can also expect to be questioned on any lack of fellowships or grants.

Q: You've never received a teaching fellowship, have you?

A: No, I have not.

Q: And you've never received a research fellowship?

A: That's right.

Q: And you've never received any research grants?

A: Correct.

Q: And your CV does not indicate that you received any awards for achievement in your field?

A: Correct. But I did receive....

Note: If the witness goes beyond her curriculum vitae, counsel will question her about the significance of the award and why it was not listed.

Professional societies

You should also expect to be questioned about any relevant professional societies or organizations to which you do not, and arguably should, belong.

Q: Now, Doctor Smith, your area of expertise is permanent impairment and disability evaluation, correct?

A: Yes.

---

[8] Robert L. Habush, *Art of Advocacy: Cross-Examination of Non-Medical Experts* (1989) 4-43.

Q: Well, now, Doctor, isn't it a fact that you do not belong the American Academy of Disability Evaluating Physicians?

A: That's true.

Q: And you do not belong to the National Association of Disability Evaluating Physicians?

A: Correct.

Q: And you are not a member of the American Board of Independent Medical Examiners?

A: That is also true.

Lack of a formal degree

In a case where there are no formal degrees granted in the area in which you claim expertise, you can expect questions like the following:[9]

Q: Mr. Smith, you claim to be an expert in exampleology, do you not?

A: Yes.

Q: Well, now, isn't it true that no college or university in the United States offers a degree in exampleology?

A: Yes, I believe that's true.

Q: And as a matter of fact, no college or university in the entire world offers a degree in exampleology?

A: Yes.

Inappropriate experience

You can also expect that the amount of experience you possess will be scrutinized during cross-examination. Counsel will often do this by attempting to show that, although you may be experienced in general, you are not experienced in the particular type of case that is the subject of the lawsuit. Consider the following:

Q: Now, sir, you have been qualified as an expert witness on automobile design, is that correct?

A: Yes.

---

[9] Harold A. Feder, *Succeeding as an Expert Witness* (1993) 163.

Q: And you have helped design over thirty different models of automobiles, right?

A: Right.

Q: But you have never designed a pick-up truck, have you?

A: Correct.

Q: And a pick-up truck is what is involved in this case, is it not?

A: Yes, it is.

When faced with a line of questioning such as this you will want to attempt to explain that the distinction between the experience you possess and the case at hand is not relevant. For instance, in the automobile design case above, the issue may have been whether a passenger-side airbag was safe for use with children under the age of 12. In response to the last question above, the expert could respond, "Yes, a pick-up truck was involved in this case. However from a design safety perspective, there is no difference between pick-up trucks and sedans when the issue is the safety of passenger-side airbags."

You should remember that frequently you will not be allowed to explain your answer during cross-examination. This is because a skilled cross-examiner will only ask you leading questions. Leading questions are designed to be answered with a simple "yes" or "no." If the judge does not allow you to explain your answers, the retaining attorney can bring out your explanations during his redirect examination of you.

Hired guns

The cross-examiner will always attempt to suggest to the jury that you are a hired gun who should not be believed. One way of doing this is by suggesting that you spend all your time consulting and testifying. As an example, consider the physician who receives all of his income through consulting work and conducting independent medical evaluations. Such a physician's credibility could easily be damaged by asking the simple question, "Doctor, when was the last time you actually treated a patient?"

Note: Expert witnesses who also teach, write, and work in the field are less subject to this type of questioning.

Lack of practical experience

You should also be prepared for the line of questioning where counsel suggests that you lack practical experience because you have spent too much time in school and too little time in the "real world." Counsel will try to diminish the weight of your testimony by suggesting that a true expert needs practical experience.[10] The following exchange illustrates this point.

> **Q:** Now, Doctor Smith, you got your PhD in business administration in 1995?
>
> **A:** Yes.
>
> **Q:** And in 1992, you received an MBA?
>
> **A:** Yes.
>
> **Q:** And you received your BA in 1990?
>
> **A:** That's correct.
>
> **Q:** And how old are you today?
>
> **A:** Twenty-eight.
>
> **Q:** Well, it seems as though you've had a lot crammed into twenty-eight years. Could you please tell us if during those twenty-eight years you have ever actually worked as a manager in a business?
>
> **A:** Well, while I was studying for my BA I was the manager of a coffee shop.

Training

You can expect counsel to use a similar technique with regard to your training. That is, counsel will attempt to distinguish the training you have had from training that would be more relevant to the issue on which you were called to testify. She will also attempt to point out obvious deficiencies in training:

> **Q:** Now, Doctor, you consider yourself an expert in disability evaluation, do you not?
>
> **A:** Yes.
>
> **Q:** And you offered this court and jury your opinion as to the disability allegedly suffered by the plaintiff?
>
> **A:** Yes, I have.
>
> **Q:** Now, Doctor, you testified during your initial questioning by counsel that you have successfully completed basic and advanced continuing medical education training courses offered by the American College of Occupational and Environmental Medicine?
>
> **A:** Yes, I have.
>
> **Q:** The courses offered by the American College of Occupational and Environmental Medicine are courses which train physicians in *impairment* evaluations, not disability evaluations, is this not correct?

---

[10] Michael E. Tigar, *Examining Witnesses* (1993) 255.

A: Yes, but they talk about disability evaluations.

Q: And isn't it a fact that as defined by the American Medical Association's *Guides to the Evaluation of Permanent Impairment* and as commonly understood, impairment evaluation and disability evaluation are different concepts?

A: Yes, they are.

Q: In fact, Doctor, you have received no specialized training on disability evaluation, have you?

If counsel is mischaracterizing your alleged lack of training you should attempt to explain this during your answers. For example, the physician above could have responded, "Yes, the titles of the American College courses refer to impairment evaluation, however, disability evaluation is also a major part of the curriculum." If you are not allowed to respond, wait for the attorney who retained you to bring out your explanations during redirect examination.

There are two additional techniques to remember when dealing with questions regarding your training. First, during direct examination, do not testify as to having completed training which supports your expertise if this training does not actually support it. Second, if it is pointed out that you have no specialized training in the area you have been called to testify about, be prepared to explain why such training is either unavailable or would not be helpful. Consider the following:

Q: OK, sir, you consider yourself an expert in the process of matching DNA in blood samples?

A: Yes.

Q: Yet, you've never received any formal training on the techniques used to identify and match DNA in blood samples, is that correct?

A: In the 1980's my colleagues at State University and I developed the techniques I used in this case. There was no training available in this science. As a matter of fact, I now train forensic experts across the country in the DNA techniques which my colleagues and I developed.

Note: Counsel would have likely attempted to cut off the explanation contained in the expert's last response.

The key, as always, is to *anticipate* counsel's questioning on your training and to *be prepared* to respond with an explanation. If you are not allowed to explain, the attorney who retained you will have an opportunity to allow you to present an explanation during redirect examination.

Missing credentials

If you are lacking in any professional credentials, you can expect this to be brought out during cross-examination.[11] Consider the following:

> **Q:** Ms. Smith, your specialty is social work, is it not?
>
> **A:** That is correct.
>
> **Q:** When you sign your name, you add the letters MSW to the end of it, that is correct?
>
> **A:** Yes.
>
> **Q:** And that signifies that you have a master's degree in social work?
>
> **A:** Yes.
>
> **Q:** Now, some social workers add the letters LISW to their names?
>
> **A:** Yes, they do.
>
> **Q:** And this indicates that they are licensed social workers?
>
> **A:** Yes, it does.
>
> **Q:** And you are not a licensed social worker, are you?
>
> **A:** No, sir, I am not.

Expert in many areas

Sometimes an attorney may attempt to discredit you by suggesting that you claim to be an expert in many different areas.[12] By showing that you are a jack of all trades, you can be easily discredited. Many engineers with general safety and design qualifications could be vulnerable to this type of attack.[13] To avoid difficulties of this kind, you should only hold yourself out to testify in cases in which you are truly qualified.

> **Q:** Mr. Smith, you are testifying today as to the safety of the design of the power saw involved in this case. I would like to show you a document. Is this a list of cases in which you have testified over the last five years in the area of expertise in which you gave your opinion?
>
> **A:** Yes, it is.
>
> **Q:** Now, over the past five years you have been qualified as an expert in a case involving a garbage disposal?
>
> **A:** Yes.

---

[11] Steven Lubet, *Modern Trial Advocacy: Analysis and Practice* (1993) 199.

[12] Robert L. Habush, *Art of Advocacy: Cross-Examination of Non-Medical Experts* (1989) 4-25.

[13] Robert L. Habush, *Art of Advocacy: Cross-Examination of Non-Medical Experts* (1989) 4-25.

Q: And a case involving a lawnmower?

A: Yes.

Q: And a case involving an airplane?

A: Yes.

Q: And a case involving a helicopter?

A: Yes.

Q: And a case involving a toaster oven?

A: Yes.

Q: And a case involving an airbag in an automobile?

A: Yes.

Q: And a case involving a gas stove?

A: Yes.

Q: And a case involving a handgun?

A: Yes.

Q: And a case involving a compressed air cylinder?

A: Yes.

Q: And a case involving a jack hammer?

A: Yes.

Q: But you have never consulted nor given testimony as to the safety of a power saw, have you?

A: No, sir, not until this case.

High profile cases

When you are involved in high profile litigation and are not certified in a specific forensic specialty, you can expect extensive questioning on your qualifications.

Typical questions include:

Q: Have you ever written a paper based on original scientific research that you designed or conducted?

Q: You are not a statistician? An engineer? An accident reconstructionist?, etc.

Here is an example of this type of cross-examination which was conducted in an all-terrain vehicle case. Note the solid responses by the expert. Note also the brevity and clarity of the expert witness' responses.

Q: Good morning.

A: Good morning.

Q: My name is Hildy Bowbeer. I'm one of the attorneys representing Honda in this litigation.

Let me ask you a few questions about your background and qualifications, if I could.

Your undergraduate degree at the University of Wisconsin, that was in history?

A: Yes, ma'am.

Q: And you've told us that your only graduate degree is in law?

A: Correct.

Q: And you're a member of several associations of attorneys, correct? Like the American Bar Association and District of Columbia Bar Association?

A: Yes, ma'am.

Q: You're also a member of the American Trial Lawyers Association, is that right?

A: Yes, ma'am.

Q: And you understand that to be an organization of trial attorneys principally directed to plaintiff's attorneys, correct?

A: Any attorney can join the Trial Lawyers Association, but I'd say that it's— there are many, many plaintiff's attorneys.

Q: OK. And you've mentioned some seminars and speeches given to attorneys' associations. Those speeches have been to seminars or conferences of the American Trial Lawyers Association or state chapters of the Trial Lawyers Association?

A: I think I gave one talk to a state chapter of the Trial Lawyers Association.

Q: And others to national conferences of the Trial Lawyers Association?

A: No, ma'am.

Q: None at all. Have you ever given a speech to any of the other professional organizations you belong to such as the Systems Safety Society or the American Society of Safety Engineers?

A: Not a speech, but I have — [14]

Q: No speeches?

A: No speeches.

Q: OK. You mentioned a couple of papers that you have written.

Have you ever written a paper based on original scientific research that you designed or conducted?

---

[14] *Note:* Once the expert replies, he is not permitted to explain.

A: I think that the work that I do is a study of technical material available; I consider that to be original.

Q: OK. That's reviewing material that's been written by other people and writing on your conclusions drawn from it?

A: That may be part of it, but some of it deals with original research such as research from the NEISS system.

Q: OK. So you've done some work with the NEISS data yourself?

A: Sure.

Q: Now, the safety management certificate that you obtained, that didn't require you to conduct research or write a paper, did it?

A: It involved taking a series of seminars.

Q: In fact, there were eight hours of seminars?

A: Eight days.

Q: Eight days of seminars. OK.

But it didn't require you to conduct original research or to write a paper?

A: No, ma'am.

Q: And you're obtaining the Certified Product Safety Manager status. That didn't require you to conduct a specific piece of original research or write a paper either, did it?

A: No, I had to take an examination.[15]

Q: OK. But it didn't require you to conduct a piece of original research as for a doctoral dissertation, for example?

A: No, it wasn't a doctoral dissertation.

Q: Not at all. Now, you indicated that your first job with the Consumer Product Safety Commission was, in fact, while you were still in law school, correct?

A: Yes, ma'am.

Q: And your title there was legal advisor, that was your title?

A: No, student assistant.

Q: Student assistant. OK. Then your first job out of law school, that is where your title became legal advisor?

A: Correct.

Q: And as I understand it, within a month or two of the time that you first became a staff member at the Consumer Product Safety Commission you had taken on responsibilities negotiating with manufacturers, is that correct?

---

[15] *Note:* The expert slips in the examination.

A: Within the first few months of my work at the Product Safety Commission, I was negotiating with actual manufactures of hair dryers.

Q: And that was while you were still in law school?

A: Yes, ma'am.

Q: And then I believe your — that position lasted for how long, I'm sorry, the time you spent as a student assistant and then continuing as a legal advisor, what length of time did that cover?

A: Well, we were a non-legal office and didn't have legal authority.

Q: But you were called a legal advisor?

A: I had a law degree at that point, that's correct.

Q: And then your last, what, about six months with the Consumer Product Safety Commission, before you left to start your own business was in the General Counsel's Office?

A: Um, yes, but that's before I went to the Institute of Safety Analysis.

Q: I'm sorry, before you went to the Institute of Safety Analysis?

A: Yes.

Q: You were in the General Counsel's Office for about six months?

A: Yes.

Q: And then there was a period in between, what, two or two-and-a-half years or —

A: Three.

Q: [Continuing] …three years that you were actually a program manager?

A: Yes.

Q: Now, you've indicated that you work with people in a variety of disciplines as a program manager?

A: Yes, ma'am.

Q: You worked with epidemiologists.

Can you tell the jury what an epidemiologist is?

A: I think, as I said before, an epidemiologist is someone who collects injury or accident or sometimes disease statistics and tries to identify trends in those areas.

Q: Now, you are not, yourself, an epidemiologist, correct?

A: That's correct.

Q: And you've taken no formal training, college courses, for example, in epidemiology, correct?

A: If you're limiting to college courses, that would be correct.

Q: OK. And you've never had any college courses in statistics either?

A: No, ma'am.

Q: And, in fact, you would not call yourself a statistician?

A: No.

Q: Now, you indicate that you supervised epidemiologists.
Did you actually have hiring and firing responsibility for the epidemiologist you worked with?

A: I could hire and fire them from my team, but not on behalf of the United States government; that was somebody else's job.

Q: In the chain of command, they reported to their superiors in the Epidemiology Directory?

A: No, that's inaccurate. The Commission had what's called a matrix management and I was their superior in order to promote the Commission's goals in hazard reduction.
They had another boss who was reviewing their epidemiological work, for example, but that work was being done at my request for me.

Q: So you would make the request for the work, but they had someone that they reported to within the Epidemiology Directory who reviewed their work in substance — on its substantive merits?

A: On its technical merits. It was my job to review their work as it was related to injury reduction.

Q: OK. But on the —

A: I wouldn't review their calculations. I would review the work to be sure it was supporting the Commission's goals in injury reduction and if it wasn't, I had the authority and responsibility to send it back.

Q: But, you are, yourself, not in the position to evaluate the technical merits of the work of an epidemiologist?

A: Not — well, not the calculations.

Q: Or even the statistical methodology. For example, if they performed a particular kind of multiple regression analysis, were you in a position to say the multiple regression analysis is not the correct analysis here?

A: Oh, that my might be my decision. I might — I might review the multiple regression analysis to make sure they did the multiples correctly.

Q: Now, you also worked with some people from the Engineering Directory?

A: Yes, ma'am.

Q: You're not an engineer yourself?

A: No.

Q: Not in any way, shape, or form, correct?

A: I have some background in engineering as it relates to safety analysis. I've taken some courses, but I'm not an engineer.

Q: You have represented in the past that you're not a design engineer?

A: Not being an engineer, I wouldn't be a design engineer either.

Q: OK. And except for the human factors engineering course which you took just this past summer —

A: Yes, ma'am.

Q: [Continuing] — you had never before taken an engineering course, is that correct?

A: That's correct.

Q: Let's see. And it look likes the last time you took mathematics was high school algebra?

A: Yeah.

Q: And let's see. You also indicated that you took this course in human factors engineering last summer before.

Before that you had not taken a course in human factors, correct?

A: I had taken some courses in communications, but not in human factors per se.

Q: And those courses in communication, there were three undergraduate courses at the University of Wisconsin that you took?

A: Correct.

Q: One of them was history of film, I believe?

A: No, it was film and communications.

Q: Film and communication. OK.

Movies, like that kind of film?

A: Yeah.

Q: OK. One of them was nonverbal communication like body language communication?

A: No, like warning.

Q: Nonverbal communication. OK. You've not indicated previously that nonverbal communication course involved body language?

A: Oh, it certainly may have, but warnings would also be a form of nonverbal communications.

Q: Nonverbal meaning not written down and not spoken?

A: It means symbols, action, words, nonverbally.

Q: OK. So it's your statement at this point that your course at the University of Wisconsin had to do with warnings?

A: I said it had to do with nonverbal communications.

That includes symbols and warnings and communications.

Q: And there was one other course, something radio and television?

A: Yes, ma'am.

Q: Those were all sort of liberal arts-type communication courses at the University of Wisconsin?

A: Communications Department.

Q: OK. You've indicated before it was part of the liberal arts curriculum at the University of Wisconsin?

A: OK.

Q: And you don't describe yourself, although you've had one course in human factors, you don't describe yourself as a human factors engineer?

A: I'm not an engineer. I have some experiences and expertise in human factors.

Q: But you don't describe yourself or present yourself to this jury as a human factors engineer?

A: Correct.

Q: You're not an accident reconstructionist?

A: No, ma'am.

Q: And you've had no formal training in accident reconstruction?

A: No, ma'am.

Q: No courses in physics?

A: No.

Q: Have you ever designed a product for sale to the public?

A: No.

Q: Have you ever designed a component of a product for sale to the public?

A: Well, when I was developing standards for the Product Safety Commission, it had that effect —

I am not an engineer. I did not do the engineering design.

Q: And you didn't actually put pen to paper and draft the blueprints for any component to be implemented or incorporated into a product, correct?

A: No, ma'am.

Q: Could you tell the jury how much time you have spent riding an all-terrain vehicle?

A: I don't ride all-terrain vehicles.

Q: You've never ridden an all-terrain vehicle, correct?

A: They're too dangerous.[16]

Q: I'm sorry. Your Honor, I'd ask the answer be stricken, it's not responsive.

    THE COURT: It's stricken from the record and the jury is instructed to disregard it.

Q: My question is you've never ever ridden an all-terrain vehicle, is that correct?

A: That's correct.

Q: Have you ever ridden an off-road motorcycle of any variety?

A: Maybe once.

Q: And I believe you've indicated in prior testimony that you may have ridden a snowmobile once?

A: I have ridden a snowmobile.

Q: OK. So you certainly don't hold yourself as an expert rider of any off-road motor vehicle of any variety, is that correct?

A: That's correct.

Q: Now, you were not employed by the Consumer Product Safety Commission during any phase of its investigation into all-terrain vehicles, correct? The current investigation that we are — that you've made reference to?

A: Not during this investigation, that's correct.

Q: OK. You were involved back in 1976 in an inquiry into throttles as I understand it?

A: That's correct.

Q: And ultimately it was decided that no corrective action was required?

A: That's correct.

Q: So your analysis of documents relating to ATVs has been since you left the CPSC and, in fact, since you've been in private practice as a consultant, correct?

A: Yes.

Q: And you indicated that much of that analysis has been principally in a litigation context?

A: Yes.

Q: And in a litigation context means that you were working for an attorney representing a plaintiff in connection with your analysis of the documents, correct?

A: As it relates to Honda cases it has been for the plaintiff.

Q: Now, let's talk just a little bit more about your training as a safety manager.

---

[16] *Note:* The expert cannot resist sticking the knife in.

You understand that there are degree programs in safety management or, for example, bachelor's degrees or master's degrees in safety management available at American universities?

A: There are now, yes.

Q: OK. It's a relatively new discipline, correct?

A: I'd say that the programs at the University is relatively new, yeah. It's not a relatively new discipline.

Q: I'm sorry. Offering the programs is a relatively new phenomenon?

A: Yes, ma'am.

Q: And one of the universities that offers both undergraduate and graduate degrees in safety management is the University of Southern California, is that correct?

A: I believe they offer a master's in safety.

Q: And do you understand that they also offer a bachelor's degree in safety?

A: I believe so. I don't know the title of it exactly but they do offer it.

Q: And you've had occasion from time to time to review their course catalog, I believe, to — and have your recollection refreshed on what courses are required in order to get that degree?

A: I've seen the catalog for a degree in safety engineering; not for safety or safety management.

Q: OK. With respect to the catalog for safety engineers, is it your recollection that you have not taken any of the courses required even as prerequisites to get into the safety engineering program?

A: Well, I don't know I could say not any, but I haven't taken the engineering courses as we've already described.

Q: Or the advanced math courses, calculus, for example?

A: That's correct.

Q: Have you ever held the title of safety manager or product safety manager in the employ of any product manufacturer?

A: I never worked for a number of product manufacturers as a —

Q: I'm sorry. My question was in the employ; employed full-time with any product manufacturer?

A: No, ma'am.

Q: Have you held that title?

A: No, ma'am.

Q: I have no further questions

Note: Despite precise questioning, the expert did not waver. He kept his replies short and to the point. Any explanations were left for redirect examination.

Chapter 3 Credibility

Challenges to Your Credibility

One major goal of counsel during cross-examination is to attempt to damage or destroy your credibility. If you are not credible, your testimony will not be believed by the jury. Assaults on credibility are most disturbing for expert witnesses (or for any witness). When responding to questions on your credibility, you must remember the rules discussed in chapter 1. Above all, tell the truth, keep calm, and don't get into an argument with counsel. The various common techniques used by counsel to question an expert witness' credibility are discussed in the following sections.

Your Fee

In most cases, the facts regarding your compensation as an expert witness will be brought out during direct examination by the attorney who retained you. This is done to lessen the impact of the opposing attorney's cross-examination.

> **Q:** Doctor, are you charging a fee for your time spent consulting on this case?
>
> **A:** Yes, I am.
>
> **Q:** And what is that fee?
>
> **A:** I am compensated at a rate of $250 an hour for out-of-court time and $300 per hour for depositions and in-court testimony.
>
> **Q:** That seems a little expensive, Doctor. How can you justify such a fee?
>
> **A:** This represents the lost income I would have received had I been seeing patients and not working as a consultant on this case.

Even if you have discussed your fee arrangements during direct examination, you can expect to be questioned closely about your fee during cross-examination. This is nothing to be ashamed of or to be nervous about. Modern juries are fairly sophisticated and you can probably assume that they realize that expert witnesses are compensated for the time they spend on a case. Also, remember that the opposing side will be paying its expert and that these lines of attack will often cancel each other out. When answering questions about your fee, remember to tell the truth and to never be smug. You should remember that, whatever your fee, it will seem to be a fortune to most members of a jury. Accordingly, you should not respond to questions about your fee in any way which would offend the jury. Consider the following example. In it the expert provides a good response to counsel's mischaracterization.

Q: Well now, Doctor, you're being paid $300 per hour for your testimony today, aren't you?

A: No, I am not. I charge a fee for my time spent consulting and in court. I am not paid for my testimony.

A common technique used by counsel is to ask you to tabulate the amount of hours that you have spent on the case. The idea is that the total fee accrued to date will be a large figure which will impress the jury.

Q: So you charge $300 dollars an hour for your time?

A: Yes.

Q: And how much time have you put into this case so far?

A: Approximately 25 hours.

Q: So, in other words, your fee for working on this case is at least $7,500?

A: Yes.

Q: And you've spent 25 hours, approximately three days' work, on this case?

A: Yes.

You must not accept any type of compensation which is contingent on the outcome of the case. Not only is this unethical, it opens you up for a very damaging cross-examination.

Q: Isn't it a fact that the compensation you have agreed upon to testify in this case amounts to 10% of any money recovered by the plaintiff?

A: Yes.

Q: And the plaintiff's attorney has retained you to testify in this case?

A: Yes.

Q: So, if the plaintiff loses, you don't get paid?

A: That's correct.

Q: And if the plaintiff wins, the more money he is awarded, the more you will get paid?

A: That is also correct.

You can also expect to be questioned as to the percentage of income you earn as an expert witness in comparison to earnings from your other endeavors. The cross-examiner will attempt to show that the proportion of income you earn as an expert witness shows that you are a hired gun who is financially dependent on expert witness work.

Q: Now, Doctor, you earned approximately $150,000 in 1995?

A: Approximately, yes.

Q: And approximately $100,000 of that money was generated as a result of your work as an expert witness in this case and others, wasn't it?

A: Yes.

Marketing Activities

One drawback to marketing activities by expert witnesses is that these efforts can be used against the expert during cross-examination. Counsel will attempt to show that you are a hired gun who actively seeks work as an expert witness and who is financially dependent on expert witness work.[1]

Q: Who first contacted you in regard to this case?

A: Robert Smith.

Q: Doesn't Robert Smith work for National Forensic Science Locator, Inc.?

A: Yes.

Q: And Mr. Smith called you on behalf of NFSL, Inc., did he not?

A: Yes, he did.

Q: Now, NFSL is a service that finds expert witnesses for attorneys, is it not?

A: Yes, it is.

Q: An attorney needs an expert in a field and he calls up NFSL, correct?

A: I would assume so.

Q: And NFSL advertises in various lawyers' publications, does it not?

A: I'm not sure.

Q: Now, sir, you have listed yourself with NFSL as an expert on the topic of helicopter design, have you not?

A: Yes, I have.

Q: And the reason you listed yourself with NFSL is so that you could get more work testifying as an expert witness, is it not?

A: Yes.

Q: Would you tell the jury about where else you advertised your services as an expert witness for hire and your other marketing efforts, sir?

The effect of this technique could be even greater if you have personally advertised yourself as being an expert witness. If you have advertised, you can expect to be confronted with a copy of the ad that you placed. Once again, counsel is attempting to suggest that you depend upon work as an expert witness.

---

[1] Robert L. Habush, *Art of Advocacy: Cross-Examination of Non-Medical Experts* (1989) 3-86.

Here is an example of this type of cross-examination.

Q: You've acted as an expert witness in fourteen cases in the last three years, have you not?

A: Yes.

Q: To promote your business of being an expert witness you regularly place an advertisement in *The Lawyers' Tribune,* do you not?

A: I am not in the business of being an expert witness, but, yes, I have on occasion placed notices in *The Lawyers' Tribune.*

Q: Is this a copy of one of the ads you occasionally placed in *The Lawyers' Tribune*?

A: Yes, it is.

Q: And this ran on October 25, 1995?

A: Apparently, yes.

Q: Could you help me out a little here? I'd like you to make sure I'm reading your ad correctly. "Walter G. Smith, PE, Consultant and Expert Witness, Over 25 Years Experience, Call 1-800-555-1234." Did I read that correctly?

A: Yes, you did.

Q: You have a toll-free number, sir?

A: I don't just use that number for this.

Q: Sir, do you have a toll-free number?

A: Yes.

Q: Now, Mr. Smith, you had to pay the publisher to place this ad in *The Lawyers' Tribune*, didn't you?

A: Of course, they don't do it for free.

Q: Didn't you in fact pay $300 for this advertisement?

A: I can't recall.

Q: And you placed an ad in every other *Lawyers' Tribune* in 1995, didn't you?

A: Yes.

Q: Is this what you meant when you said you occasionally place an ad in *The Lawyers' Tribune*?

A: Yes.

Q: So, over the course of 1995 you spent almost $1,700 to advertise in *The Lawyers' Tribune*?

A: Yes.

Q: Now, Mr. Smith, let's talk a little bit about the other publications that you advertise in and the Web page you had constructed on the Internet to advertise your expert witness business.

A: OK.

Q: The Internet is used by millions of people each day is it not?

Note: Experienced expert witnesses are very cautious about how they market their services. Being too aggressive can negatively affect your credibility and eventually negatively affect your expert witness practice.

Relationship to Retaining Party or Attorney

You should expect counsel to question you to attempt to show that your relationship with the retaining party or attorney, or your relationship with other entities, makes you a biased or unreliable witness. Consider this example where counsel attempts to imply that the witness is partial to the defendant.

> **Q:** Now, sir, isn't it a fact that you have testified on behalf of the defendant in this case, Acme Pharmacueticals, twenty-seven times over the last ten years?
>
> **A:** Yes, it is.
>
> **Q:** And isn't is also a fact that you have earned over $250,000 for this testimony?

Counsel may also attempt to suggest to the jury that because you have testified for the same attorney or party in the past, you are biased because you may seek future employment with them as an expert witness.

> **Q:** Now, Doctor, you've been retained by Mr. Jones' law firm to testify in seven cases over the last three years, haven't you?
>
> **A:** That is correct.
>
> **Q:** And the fees you have charged for those seven cases total approximately $70,000, correct?
>
> **A:** Yes.
>
> **Q:** OK, Doctor, now you wouldn't want to risk your comfortable deal here with Mr. Jones by saying anything here today which might hurt his case, would you?[2]

If you are related to one of the parties or one of the attorneys, this will also be brought out. The same is true if it can be shown that you are friends with one of the parties. If this is the case, inform your retaining attorney immediately. If you are

---

[2] See *Collins v. Wayne Corp.*, 621 F.2d 777 (5th Cir. 1980).

questioned about your relationship to the parties, admit the relationship and don't make it appear to be a bigger problem than it actually is. Don't try to be coy or evasive because the cross-examining attorney will get to the truth and will be able to emphasize your potential bias.

> **Q:** Isn't it a fact, Doctor, that you and Mr. Smith, the plaintiff's attorney, are good friends?
>
> **A:** Well, I wouldn't call us good friends.
>
> **Q:** You wouldn't? Well, isn't it a fact that you graduated from State University together?
>
> **A:** Yes.
>
> **Q:** And isn't it also a fact that you attended Mr. Smith's daughter's wedding last year?
>
> **A:** Yes.
>
> **Q:** And didn't you send him a Christmas card last year?
>
> **A:** Yes, I did.[3]

The lesson here is not to try to outsmart the examining attorney. If you are good friends with the attorney who retained you, then admit it. Appearing to be evasive will only make things worse. One final example follows:

> **Q:** So, Doctor, is it your testimony that the defendant was not negligent and did not commit medical malpractice?
>
> **A:** Yes.
>
> **Q:** You belong to the Twin Oaks Country Club, don't you?
>
> **A:** Yes, I do.
>
> **Q:** There are about 250 members of that club, correct?
>
> **A:** About that, yes.
>
> **Q:** Now, Doctor, isn't the defendant, Dr. Jones, also a member at Twin Oaks?
>
> **A:** Yes, he is.

> *Note:* In this example the attorney was attempting to show a subtle bias toward the witness' club mate.

Affiliation with an Insurance Company

If, as an expert witness, you are affiliated with, or have been affiliated with, the insurance carrier involved in the matter being litigated, you can expect to be questioned about this

---

[3] See *Treece v. Greyhound Bus Co.*, 234 N.W.2d 404 (Mich. App. 1975).

affiliation. For example, see the case of *Golden v. Kishwaukee Com. Health Serv.*, 645 N.E. 2d 319 (Ill. App. 1 Dist. 1994), in which the court found that a physician could be cross-examined about his membership in a mutual medical malpractice insurance program.

The court stated:

> In the instance of Dr. C., Dr. B.'s expert, who testified in his behalf and, incidentally, favorably for Kishwaukee, Dr. C. was shown to have more than a cursory interest in this case. Dr. C. performed significant economic services for the Exchange in reviewing claims made against the Exchange's doctor members to determine if those suits should have any impact on the insurance premiums they pay. The possibility of some significant question of bias exceeding potential prejudice should have been recognized by the court in this instance. The benefit to the Exchange in premium adjustments that take place is ineluctable.

Here is an example of the type of cross-examination that can be expected regarding insurance company affiliations:

Q: To your knowledge, have you ever testified or reviewed for CAP/MPT before?

A: Yes.

Q: How many times?

A: About ten, I would say.

Q: OK. Would that be directly for the carrier itself or for the insurance company — or for defense firms retained by that carrier?

A: Both.

Q: OK. So you — so CAP/MPT has sent you cases, true?

A: Correct.

Q: Is that your carrier?

A: Correct.

Q: How long have you been insured by CAP/MPT?

A: I believe we started in 1978.

Q: OK. And you have been with them ever since?

A: Correct.

Q: Have you sat on the board at CAP?

A: I have been on the Claims Review Committee for Orange County.

Q: OK. Are you still on that committee?

A: I am not.

Q: OK. When were you on the Claims Review Committee for Orange County for CAP?

A: I believe I started serving in approximately 1979 or 1980 and terminated in approximately 1986 or 1987.

Q: And what did you do as a member of the claims committee of CAP?

A: Do you want me to describe how that — how it functions or —

Q: Just — year, basically what you did with it. I'm pretty well aware of how it functions.

A: Well, we met monthly. Prior to each meeting they send a large claims review book, so we are expected to be familiar with all of the cases. Although, if time did not permit reading the entire case book, we were expected to at least be familiar with the cases in our specialty. Then we would review the cases at the meeting, and you said you were already familiar with the format of the claims review?

Q: Yes.

OK. Why did you cease your duties with the claims committee?

A: Well, from my side, it was because I was tired of going to it. From their side, I think they wanted to bring some fresh blood in.

Conversations with Retaining Attorney

Since the attorney who has retained you is not your attorney, conversations between you and your retaining attorney are not protected by the attorney-client privilege. You can expect such conversations to be explored during cross-examination.[4]

Q: Now, during your work on this case you have met with Attorney Jones on more than one occasion have you not?

A: Yes.

Q: And you have spoken with him on the phone several times?

A: That's correct.

Q: And during these conversations, did not Attorney Jones tell you what opinion he was seeking from you in 'this case?

A: He did.

Q: And it is Attorney Jones who is paying your fee of $300 per hour, is it not?

A: Yes, he is.

Q: Oh, and didn't Attorney Jones meet with you before this trial to go over your testimony here today?

A: Yes.

---

[4] Richard A. Givens, *Advocacy: The Art of Pleading a Cause* (1992) 153.

Q: How many hours did that meeting take?

You can also be expected to be questioned about conversations and offhand remarks made to your retaining counsel in and around the courthouse. As can be seen from the following example, it is wise to avoid such remarks.

Q: Doctor, isn't it a fact that while leaving court yesterday, you said to Attorney Smith, in reference to me, and I quote, "Don't worry about it. We'll shove it to him"?[5]

Indirect Monetary Interest

As the next exchange illustrates, counsel could also attempt to show that you have an indirect monetary interest in the outcome of the case.[6]

Q: Now, Doctor, you have just testified on behalf of the defendant, RJR Nabisco, that nicotine is not addictive, have you not?

A: Yes, I have.

Q: Now isn't it a fact, Doctor, that you own over $150,000 worth of stock in Philip Morris, another big cigarette manufacturer?

A: I don't know exactly how much it is worth.

Q: And isn't it also true, that should the value of your Philip Morris stock decrease, you would suffer a decrease in your net worth?

Consider the following as well.

Q: I see from your curriculum vitae, Doctor, that your are president of Smith & Associates, Inc., a private think tank. Is that correct?

A: Yes, I am.

Q: Well, now, Doctor, isn't it a fact that over the last five years Smith & Associates has received over $200,000 in funding from the tobacco industry, including $50,000 from the defendant in this case, to support research into the effects of tobacco smoking?

A: Yes, that is correct.

---

[5] See *LeBlanc v. Lettini,* 266 N.W.2d 643 (Mich. App. 1978).
[6] Richard A. Givens, *Advocacy: The Art of Pleading a Cause* (1992) 153.

Prior Testimony

Counsel will attempt to use any of your prior testimony to impeach your credibility, that is, to discredit you. One technique counsel will use is to attempt to paint you as a hired gun expert witness. Consider the following example. In it, counsel suggests that the witness always has the same opinion, regardless of the facts of the case. He is trying to show that the physician is merely a hired gun for defense attorneys.

> **Q:** Now, Doctor, you were retained by the defense to conduct a physical examination of the plaintiff and to render your opinion as to the level of physical impairment suffered by the plaintiff?
>
> **A:** That's correct.
>
> **Q:** And you did in fact conduct a fifteen-minute physical examination of the plaintiff?
>
> **A:** Yes.
>
> **Q:** And haven't you testified just now on direct examination that it is your opinion that the plaintiff is not suffering any permanent impairment?
>
> **A:** That's right, he has no permanent impairment.
>
> **Q:** Now in the past five years, Doctor, you've been retained as an expert witness seventeen times, isn't that correct?
>
> **A:** Approximately, yes.
>
> **Q:** And in each of these seventeen cases you were retained by the defense, weren't you?
>
> **A:** Yes, I was.
>
> **Q:** And in each and every one of these cases, isn't it a fact that your opinion was that the plaintiff suffered no physical impairment?
>
> **A:** Yes.
>
> **Q:** In fact, Doctor, over the twenty years you have been testifying you have only testified once on behalf of a plaintiff, is that correct?
>
> **A:** Yes.

> *Note:* If counsel can show that you are a hired gun for either plaintiffs or defendants, your credibility will be destroyed. It is completely legitimate for counsel to ask what cases you have worked on in the past, who retained you, and what your opinion was. To avoid being labeled as a hired gun, and thus destroying your viability as an expert witness, you should strive to make yourself available to be retained by both plaintiffs and defendants. You should also avoid testifying too frequently.

Counsel will probe any prior testimony you have given in other cases to search for inconsistencies with your current testimony. Your prior testimony is becoming easily available to opposing attorneys. Currently, many organizations maintain deposition and trial testimony transcript banks. Some transcripts are even available online.

You must assume that counsel has access to any and all of the prior testimony you have given in previous cases. If you have made any prior testimony that could reasonably be construed as being inconsistent with your current testimony, you should immediately bring this fact to retaining counsel's attention. If you do not, the results could be devastating.[7]

> **Q:** Now, Doctor, you have just stated your opinion that nicotine is addictive, correct?
>
> **A:** Yes.
>
> **Q:** Do you recall testifying in the case of *Smith v. Jones* in Central District Court on May 27, 1995?
>
> **A:** Yes, I do.
>
> **Q:** And isn't it a fact that on that occasion you testified that nicotine was not addictive?

> *Note:* If counsel is mischaracterizing your prior testimony, you should be prepared to explain the previous testimony. It could be that he has taken your prior testimony out of context. Another possibility is that the state of knowledge in your field has evolved such that, although your prior opinion was valid at the time, your current opinion is different. In any case, you and your retaining counsel must be ready to explain any prior testimony which appears to be inconsistent. This explanation can be done on cross-examination, if possible, or during redirect examination. If you are not prepared to offer a credible explanation for the inconsistency, your credibility will be greatly damaged.

If you have been deposed, you can expect counsel to use the transcript of your deposition testimony to highlight any apparent inconsistencies with your testimony at trial. You can also expect counsel to have access to transcripts from depositions you have given in other cases.

> **Q:** Mr. Smith, you have given your opinion that, based upon the blood alcohol level taken by the police officers, that the defendant's ability to properly and safely operate a motor vehicle was impaired. Is that your opinion?
>
> **A:** Yes.
>
> **Q:** And you have been retained by the prosecution in this case?
>
> **A:** Yes.
>
> **Q:** Do you recall giving a deposition in the civil case of *Manta v. Jones*?

---

[7] Harold A. Feder, "Methods of Challenging Forensic Fraud and Unethical Behavior," *Shepard's Expert and Scientific Evidence Quarterly* 2, no. 4 (Spring 1995) 2.

A: Ah, yes.

Q: And in that case, you were retained by the defendant?

A: Yes.

Q: And that case involved a motor vehicle accident?

A: Yes, I believe it did.

Q: And the defendant was accused of being negligent by operating his vehicle while under the influence of alcohol?

A: Yes.

Q: I'm going to read from the deposition transcript of the deposition you gave in the *Manta* case, with reference to page 24 starting at line 10.

A: Fine.

Q: And the deposition you gave at that time was under oath?

A: Yes, of course.

Q: And you are under oath here today?

A: Yes.

Q: Question, "Is it possible to determine whether a person's ability to operate a motor vehicle is impaired, based solely on a blood alcohol measurement taken at a later time?" Your answer was, "No."

Am I reading that correctly?

The expert in the above example should be prepared to explain the apparent inconsistency of his opinions. He will probably be given an opportunity to explain during redirect examination.

The most potentially damaging cross-examination regarding prior testimony is the direct attack on your opinion. For example:

Q: You've testified in the past that physicians fell below the standard of care, haven't you?

A: Of course.

Q: So, you would agree that on occasion that can happen?

A: Yes.

Q: Well, Doctor, you've testified in the past that doctors don't always do the things you would expect them to do.

A: But this is reflex, fundamental.

Q: But you've testified in the past that trained people sometimes don't do what they're supposed to do, is that right? You'd agree, wouldn't you?

A: Yes, yes. It's a non sequitur.

Q: You have testified in the past that intubation caused bronchiospasm, right?

A: Oh, sure.

Here is another example of impeachment with prior testimony. In this example, the expert's answers to written interrogatories are used to impeach him.

Q: Now, I understand, Doctor, that it is your contention in this case that the claimant has Guillian-Barre Syndrome, is that right?

A: No, I don't believe I ever said I thought he had Guillian-Barre Syndrome. This is a suggestion made by a neurologist as a possible cause of this.

Q: I have to apologize, Doctor. I am mistaken.

A: Maybe a year ago I may have said that, but I don't recall saying that.

Q: May I approach your honor?

THE COURT: Yes, you may.

Q: Is that your signature, sir?

A: Yes.

Q: What is the date?

A: 26th October 1995.

Q: And this says, "State of California, County of Orange. I have read the foregoing defendant's further responses to plaintiff's special interrogatories set one and know its contents"?

A: Yes.

Q: "I am a party to this action. The matter stated in the foregoing document is true to my own knowledge, except as to those matters which are stated on information and belief and as to those matters, I believe them to be true. I declare under penalty of perjury, under the laws of the State of California that the foregoing is true and correct." Is that what it says?

A: Yes.

Q: OK. Now, then, if you were verifying these interrogatory responses under penalty of perjury I presume you read them, sir?

A: I probably did, yes.

Q: OK. Now, question number 8 was this: "State precisely how you contend plaintiff received the injury he is alleging in the lawsuit."

Read the last sentence in your response.

MS. T.: Objection, your Honor. It is a total response.

Q: Read the whole response.

A: "Without waiving defendants' prior objection to this interrogatory, defendants state that the precise etiology of plaintiff's alleged injuries are unknown, but contend that plaintiff's diabetic condition and pre-existing neuropathy contributed to his present condition. Defendants further contend that plaintiff's injuries occurred in the absence of any negligence. Defendants contend that plaintiff's injuries are the result of a post-infectious process affecting the nervous system, commonly known as Guillian-Barre Syndrome."

Q: Now, when you declared that to be true under penalty of perjury, Doctor Wawro, did you mean it?

A: Well, no, not really.

Note: As might be expected, this was not a satisfactory response.

Professional Presentations

When you have given professional presentations you can expect to be cross-examined about these presentations. Attorneys will be looking for ammunition to challenge your opinion and to see if they can unearth conflicting statements you might have made previously.

A typical "fishing expedition" in this area is as follows:

Q: Now, do you know whether or not that presentation in 1987 was recorded or filmed?

A: It was not.

Q: To whom did you make the presentation?

A: I was a visiting professor at the Southern Illinois University School of Medicine in Springfield, Illinois. That presentation was given to orthopedic residents as well as to several orthopedic attendants. The exact number of attendants and the exact number of residents I'm not sure of, probably less than twenty.

Q: Do you know the subject — do you know the gist or substance of the presentation that you made which was entitled, "External Fixation with Skeletal Injuries"?

A: It basically dealt with a method of fixing fractures known as external fixation.

Q: In that presentation did you discuss the relative advantages of external fixation over internal fixation of a particular injury?

A: When you say internal fixation —

Q: Use of a rod and screws.

A: I don't know if I specifically compared those two methods. Upon giving a talk such as that I point out the pros and cons of that method.

Q: Have you — do you know whether the talk itself has been published anywhere?

A: No, it has not.

Q: Now, in 1989 you gave a presentation, "Bone Transport for Tibial Non-Unions with Bone Defect." Do you recall to whom you made that presentation?

A: Again, that was in Springfield, Illinois while I was an attending physician at the Southern Illinois University School of Medicine. That was given again to residents, I believe, therapists, medical students.

Q: Do you have any notes or outlines or writings of that presentation?

A: Again, it would be in the form of 35-millimeter slides that may or may not all be together in that original talk.

Q: Again, I'll request that if you have any of those slides related to that topic, if you would hold on to those and I'll make a formal written request through your counsel for copies of that.

On your fourth page of Exhibit 1, you list acknowledgments, what do you consider an acknowledgment?

A: Just for a completeness of the CV. In the *Journal of Orthopedic Trauma* their volume 3, number 2, an article was published regarding flexible intramedullary nailing of adolescent femoral shaft fractures, in that article my name was mentioned. My patients in particular were used as one of the primary sources of clinical material for that article.

Q: So you were not the author or one of the researchers, were you, of that?

A: No.

Q: Have you had any other articles published in any professional journals?

A: There may be an article that, as I stated earlier, that is going to be published sometime in the near future, I'm not sure which journal or which book or whatever. I'm the second author, that is my understanding.

Q: Do you know where the primary author of the — the resident now lives?

A: Somewhere in Connecticut, I could get that information for you.

Professional and Personal Writings

You may need to be wary of any of your prior writings. This is especially true of articles and texts which you have published. With modern electronic research tools, it is very easy for counsel to obtain copies of what you have published, even if you have omitted these publications from your CV. Counsel will dig into your writings to attempt to find any opinion or assumption which contradicts your opinion in the case at hand. Again, you and your retaining attorney must be prepared to explain these discrepancies or you should not testify in the case.

Q: Now, Doctor, isn't it a fact that you authored an article called "Nicotine Addiction" which was published in the medical journal *Substance Abuse* in February 1994?

A: Yes.

Q: And isn't it a fact that in the article you stated that no credible scientific evidence existed that nicotine was addictive?

A: That's correct. However, today that evidence does exist and it has been recognized and accepted by me and the majority of the scientific community.

Here is another example.

Q: Now, Doctor, you just testified that it is highly unlikely for exposure to chemical x to cause breast cancer, is that correct?

A: Yes.

Q: Do you recall writing an article on chemical x exposure published in *Scientific Quarterly* in June of 1995?

A: Yes, I do.

Q: Is this a copy of that article?

A: Yes, it is.

Q: Could you please read for the jury the last sentence of the third full paragraph on page 11?

A: "It can therefore be concluded that there is a causal relationship between exposure to chemical x and breast cancer."

Here is another example of questioning on prior writings. Here, the examining attorney points out that the article in question was never actually published.

Q: Now, you also indicated that you had authored a book on the design of wing tip fuel tanks, published by Stanford University.

A: Yes. And I no longer list that, because the book did not get published. At the time I made this out it was planned to be published, but it never was.

Q: That was never published. So that was an error?

A: No, that wasn't an error. The book — all right. Let's go into some details, then. The book was being edited by some book firm that was going to publish the book, but for some financial reason the book was not published. Now, that had nothing to do with my experience or what I did with the book or what I wrote in the book. That was a financial problem.

Q: But you told the FAA in that resume, quote, "I authored a book on design of wing tip fuel tanks, published by Stanford University"?

A: That was the publisher, and I was the author.

Q: Was it ever published?

A: No, it did not get published because of financial problems.

Q: But you told the FAA that you had published it?

A: What I'm saying is, the book — I wrote the book; it didn't get published.

Q: Why did you put on here, "Published by ...."?

A: I'm telling you who the company is that's publishing it, that's all.

Q: Did they publish it?

A: It did not get into print, but they are the publishers. I understand the term publisher meaning the company that manufactures books. And what I'm saying is that is the company that was going to publish the book.

Note: The expert's evasive responses make a bad situation even worse.

Consider this final example, where the expert's opinion is attacked directly.

Q: Have you ever written anywhere that a concentration of more than 2% Halothane for a maintenance dose can cause impending cardiovascular collapse?

A: It's possible. I've written a lot of things. It depends on the circumstances.

Note: If the expert had answered no in this last example, and he had in fact written what he was asked, he could then expect to be confronted with a copy of the writing(s) in question.

You must also beware of your prior writings that may not have been published. Have you written letters to the editor or internal memoranda that could prove damaging? Counsel will dig, especially in significant cases, to locate and obtain any and all documents which you have written. Finally, remember that anything you have written is arguably discoverable and counsel has subpoena powers to obtain these documents from either you or from third parties. Beware and be prepared.

Challenges to Your Opinion

Your Opinion's Foundation

The foundation of your opinion is the facts upon which that opinion is based. These foundational facts will usually be in dispute and will be heatedly debated during the litigation. Counsel will attempt to disprove the facts on which each expert opinion is based, in an attempt to discredit the opinion.

You can expect counsel to cross-examine you regarding these foundational facts. Counsel usually uses common techniques to do this. In each case, however, the attorney is trying to make the point to the jury that your opinion is less credible if it is based upon erroneous or incomplete facts. In any event, counsel will usually precede questioning along these lines with an inquiry as to which facts and documents your opinion is based on.

> **Q:** Could you please tell the jury what documents and other materials you reviewed when forming your opinion?

This is a legitimate area of inquiry and you should be prepared to respond fully and accurately. Another related question would be as follows:

> **Q:** Doctor, could you please summarize the plaintiff's medical history as you understand it?

You must once again be prepared to answer fully and accurately. Failure to do so will suggest to the jury that you are not familiar with the underlying facts upon which your opinion is based.

Often, counsel will ask you if you considered a specific document when forming your opinion.[8] Counsel will then attempt to show that the document in question contained a key relevant fact that you overlooked. If he is successful, he can show that your opinion is based upon incomplete facts.

> **Q:** Now, Doctor, in preparation for your testimony in this case, did you review the annual reports for X Corporation for 1994 and 1995?
>
> **A:** No, I did not.
>
> **Q:** And did you review the internal memorandum from John Hughes, President of X Corp., dated October 25, 1995?
>
> **A:** No.

---

[8] Michael E. Tigar, *Examining Witnesses* (1993) 237-238.

Q: And did you study any of the reports on X Corporation prepared by the Federal Trade Commission?

A: No.

Q: Did you ever review any document in this case that was not given to you by Attorney Jones?

A: No.

Q: Would your review of these documents have changed your opinion in this case?

Note: If the expert says yes, his opinion is in jeopardy. If he says no, he will be questioned about how he could be sure because he has not seen the documents in question.

Forensic expert witnesses can expect to be cross-examined about what they relied upon in formulating their opinions on causation. Counsel will attempt to get the expert witness to comment on areas such as the extent of physical injuries. Once the expert leaves her domain, any mistakes she makes could undermine her credibility and even the foundation of her opinion.

Here is an example of such an attempt:

Q: Doctor, your opinion is not based in any manner upon the injury patterns that the three people in the vehicle suffered, is that correct?

A: Well, the injury is affected, but I'm not an expert who can explain the detail of what kind of injury is caused by what part of the vehicle, but it's very consistent.

Q: So, in forming your opinion, you do look at the injuries to make sure they are consistent with what your theory is, is that correct?

A: That's correct.

Q: OK. And what is your understanding of the injuries that the claimant received as a result of this accident?

A: It will be a very minor injury if he had a seat belt, because the impact is to the rear, and if he didn't have a seat belt, then he will suffer more injuries, because he would go back and hit the roof and windshield and door and the steering wheel and everything.

Q: Now, if the rear passenger was belted in, you would also say that he would have minor injuries, is that correct?

A: Right.

Q: So, although you wouldn't be comfortable testifying strictly as to injury patterns and how those affect your opinion, injury patterns do play somewhat into your opinion, is that correct?

A: Oh, yes.

Q: But when you say you couldn't testify to that, you couldn't testify specifically what type of injury should occur when part of your body hits the steering wheel, is that correct?

A: Well, I am not very comfortable to testify, because I'm not medically trained. If I had MD degrees, then probably I could be more specific, but since I don't have that background I don't feel very comfortable to say.

Q: So not specific injuries, but sort of generally, what type of injuries would have occurred? You're more comfortable with giving your opinion in those terms?

A: Right, that's fine.

Q: And if someone is ejected from the vehicle who does not have a seat belt on, you would anticipate severe injuries to that person, is that correct?

A: Without seat belt — was ejected from — oh, yes. Oh, yes, because of speed.

Reliance on Tests Not Personally Performed

Often your opinion will be based upon tests which you have not personally performed. Although it is permissible for you to rely on tests you have not performed yourself, your opinion may be given less weight when this is the case. You can expect counsel to highlight the tests upon which you relied which you did not personally perform.[9]

Q: You never personally examined the plaintiff, did you, Doctor Jones?

A: No, I did not.

Q: And as you stated previously, your testimony is based upon the medical records of the plaintiff that you have reviewed, is that correct?

A: Yes.

Q: Now, among these records is a radiological report dated 11/1/96?

A: Yes, there is.

Q: Doctor, did you ever review the x-rays upon which this radiological report was based?

A: No.

Q: Your opinion is based in part on the findings of the radiological report correct?

A: Yes.

Q: You don't know from first-hand knowledge that the report is accurate, do you, Doctor?

---

[9] Roberto Aron et al., *Cross-Examination of Witnesses: The Litigator's Puzzle* (1989) 331.

A: That is correct.

Q: And the lab report dated 11/1/96 detailing the plaintiff's blood test. Were you there when this test took place?

A: No.

Q: Do you know if the lab followed proper procedures when analyzing the plaintiff's blood sample?

A: I don't know.

Note: When you rely on records of others in testifying, it is crucial that retaining counsel lay a proper foundation for the reliance on these records during direct examination.

Reliance on Other Experts' Records

As an expert witness you may, on occasion, rely on the reports of other experts in formulating your opinion and testimony. For example, a physician frequently relies upon the reports of other physicians, particularly in the area of medical testing, to assist in formulating his opinion. This is permitted under Rule 703 of the Federal Rules of Evidence.[10] A typical exchange follows:

Q: Doctor, would you look at these three pages, being radiology, CAT scan, and myelogram reports from December of 1988? Would you just familiarize yourself with those reports?

A: OK.

Q: And have you familiarized yourself with the other two reports, one being a report of a CAT scan and report of a lumbar myelogram in December of '88, and one being a report of a lumbar spine without contrast in May of '88?

A: Yes. I have read both of these.

Q: Are you familiar with that type of document?

A: Yes.

Q: Is that type of report used by practicing physicians in the practice of medicine?

A: Yes, it is.

Q: For what purpose?

A: In formulating a diagnosis and in formulating a treatment plan.

Q: The doctors who prepare these reports, are they specialists in the field of reading and interpreting the CAT scan and the myelogram-type test?

---

[10] See Appendix C.

A: Yes.

Q: And in the practice of medicine, is it your experience that physicians customarily will rely on such reports while treating patients or examining patients?

A: Yes.

Q: Doctor, having reviewed the CAT scan and myelogram reports from December of 1988, does anything contained in there in any way change the opinion you stated previously as to the plaintiff's physical condition?

A: No.

Q: Doctor, have you just had a chance to review your findings of January 23, 1990 with the findings stated in the myelogram report of 12/9/88?

A: Yes. I have reviewed both of those pieces of information.

Q: And with respect to the findings of prominent nerve root filling defect at level L5-S1 interspace, as on the myelogram of 12/9/88, is that finding consistent or inconsistent with your clinical findings on physical examination of January 23 of 1988?

A: That's consistent with the physical findings noted on the examination of January 23, 1990.

Q: Thank you, Doctor.

Doctor, you weren't benefited with this myelogram at the time of your examination, is that correct?

A: That is correct.

Q: And your opinion as to the consistency between the myelogram and your report has been made with a very brief opportunity to review the myelogram and the report itself, correct?

A: With an opportunity to read the report of the myelogram, but not review the myelogram itself, and with extensive review of my report.

Reliance on Self-Reported History

When your testimony as an expert witness is based solely on a self-reported history you can anticipate the following line of questioning.

Q: On what history did you base your opinion, Doctor?

A: Mr. Dukes sat with me and I asked him about the activities that he engaged in and the onset of his symptoms back when he had the carpal tunnel syndrome, and he described activities to me. And, at that time, I formed a judgment that such activities could have caused the problem or aggravated an underlying condition.

Q: If the history that Mr. Dukes provided you is not accurate, would that affect the reliability of your clinical judgment that's based upon that inaccurate history?

A: It is possible, yes.

Omitted Facts

One way counsel will challenge the foundation of your testimony is through attempting to show that you did not consider or improperly omitted relevant facts when forming your opinion. For example, assume you are a physician who has given your opinion that the plaintiff's back condition was caused by an automobile accident. Counsel may bring to your attention the fact that the plaintiff suffered a previous severe injury to his back when slipping in a supermarket two years prior to the automobile accident.

Q: Doctor, you have testified on direct examination that the plaintiff's back injury was caused by his 11/1/96 automobile accident, have you not?

A: That is correct.

Q: In reaching that opinion, Doctor, were you aware of the fact that the plaintiff had previously suffered a back injury as a result of a slip and fall on 11/1/94?

A: No, I was not so aware.

Q: Where did you get the medical history in this case from, Doctor?

A: From the patient.

Q: He didn't tell you about the slip and fall in 11/94?

A: That is not reflected in my notes.

Q: OK, Doctor, let's assume for the moment that the plaintiff did indeed suffer a back injury as a result of a slip and fall injury on 11/1/94, wouldn't that fact be important in your determining the cause of his current back condition?

A: It could be.

You should always be wary of the trap posed by the following type of question.

Q: Now, Doctor, if there were other medical records of the plaintiff which you were not aware of at the time of your evaluation, would you have preferred to have reviewed these records before forming your opinion as to the cause of the plaintiff's back injury?

Your answer to these types of questions must always be affirmative because you would have preferred to have reviewed all the records. The next question is obvious.

Q: Well, Doctor, had you reviewed the other medical records of the plaintiff, would it have changed your opinion?

At this point counsel has put you on the spot. The most proper answer is, "It would depend on what is in the records," as you do not know what is in these hypothetical records. In any event, counsel will be able to suggest to the jury that your opinion was based upon incomplete information. The way to prepare for these types of questions is to do everything possible to make sure that you have reviewed all key documentary evidence. If documentary evidence appears to be missing, let your retaining attorney know and insist on having such evidence before you testify.

Many times, due to time pressures by retaining counsel, expert witnesses will issue their reports without the benefit of having all the relevant data. Expect to be cross-examined about why you did not have the data and whether the data would have assisted you or altered your opinion in any way. For example in the case of *American and Foreign Ins. Co. v. General Electric Co.,* 45 F.3d 135 (6th Cir. 1995), an electrical engineer's testimony was excluded in a product liability case.

> During the hearing he was asked to produce all of his notes relating to the test itself and any protocol established for the test. He responded that he had not established any protocol, that he had taken no notes during the testing, and that he had discarded the "raw data," i.e., the numbers he read on the oscilloscope screen. He also testified that, although calibration of testing equipment was important to insure accurate readings, he was unsure whether his testing equipment had been calibrated. Finally, he testified that no one had witnessed the test and that the only evidence he had of the test was a single slip of paper consisting of a summary graph of the results.

Following is a brief example of how counsel can and will utilize a lack of data to his advantage. As you can see, an admission of not having needed data can be very damaging.

Q: Down at the bottom of one of the drafts it appears to say you need, one, apartment dimensions; two, number and position of windows. You never got that data either?

A: No.

Q: So that was information you deemed relevant to rendering your report?

A: Yes.

Q: That's information you did not obtain prior to rendering your report.

A: Right.

Q: Correct? And, nonetheless, you went ahead and proceeded to express an opinion to a reasonable degree of scientific certainty without that relevant information?

A: That is correct.

Hypothetical Questions

Counsel may also present you with hypothetical facts and attempt to determine whether these facts could have changed your opinion.[11] With the adoption of Federal Rule 705 counsel is no longer required to present every essential fact into evidence before the expert can express her opinion. Thus, the need for hypothetical questions during direct examination is substantially reduced. However, hypothetical questions remain a favorite method of cross-examination.

> One of the most frequently employed methods of conducting a frontal attack on an expert's opinion is to ask hypothetical questions. Hypothetical questions on cross-examination provide the opportunity to test the learning, experience, skill, and expertise of the witness. Indeed, use of such questions may be an opportunity to prove that the expert's opinions are not reasonable or logical. Preparation of a hypothetical should be performed with the assistance of one's own expert.[12]

Counsel will usually ask the expert to remove or change key facts and ask if this would change her opinion. When the expert refuses to change her opinion even after the facts are changed she appears biased. The best way to anticipate these questions is to go over in detail the other side's theory of the case with your retaining attorney. If the other side claims that certain facts exist that the party retaining you denies, this is the probable area of inquiry. Insist on obtaining complete records.

> **Q:** Sir, haven't you just testified on direct that the flight in question crashed due to a catastrophic mechanical failure?
>
> **A:** Yes.
>
> **Q:** Now, sir, let's assume for a moment that immediately before the flight in question crashed, a surface-to-air missile had been fired at the plane, and this missile struck the plane and exploded. Would that fact change your opinion as to the cause of the failure of the flight?

This type of questioning can be prepared for by understanding the other side's theory of the case. In this case, the theory is that the flight in question was shot down by a surface-to-air missile, and that it did not crash due to mechanical failure.

Remember that in many cases your opinion certainly could change if the omitted facts were found to have occurred. If this is the case, testify that your opinion could be changed. It is generally not your job or role to determine which facts are correct. That is up to the lawyers and, ultimately, the jury. In any event, when confronted with a complex hypothetical question, take your time before answering.[13]

---

[11] Roberto Aron et al., *Cross-Examination of Witnesses: The Litigator's Puzzle* (1989) 328.
[12] Roberto Aron et al., *Cross-Examination of Witnesses: The Litigator's Puzzle* (1989) 328.
[13] Jack V. Matson, *Effective Expert Witnessing* (Lewis Publications: 1990) 57.

> **Q:** Let me ask you a hypothetical question….
>
> **A:** I need some time to consider your hypothetical, Mr. Jones. I cannot respond immediately.

Erroneous Facts

Another way to challenge your opinion is to highlight the importance of the facts which you relied upon when forming your opinion. Counsel will then present you with hypothetical variations of these facts in an attempt to suggest that, were these hypothetical facts true, your opinion would be discredited. Again, the hypothetical facts that counsel is most likely to present will be based upon facts which fit with his side's theory of the case. You can prepare for these questions by learning the other side's theory from the attorney who retained you.

> **Q:** Sir, isn't it a fact that you based your opinion as to the plaintiff's life expectancy on the assumption that the plaintiff was a non-smoker?
>
> **A:** Yes, it is.
>
> **Q:** Let's assume for the moment that the plaintiff has a fifty pack-year history of smoking cigarettes, and the plaintiff continues to smoke one pack of cigarettes per day. Wouldn't this information alter your opinion as to the life expectancy of the plaintiff?

In such a situation, all you need do is answer the question. Yes, if the plaintiff was a smoker, it might change your opinion. Remember, it is generally *not* your task to resolve whether the plaintiff was in fact a smoker. This is something that the attorneys can argue over. It *is* your job to obtain as much information as you can and to base your opinion on that information. A skillful cross-examiner may attempt to question you in the following way:

> **Q:** Now, Doctor, you have no interest in helping either side win this case, you are simply giving your best opinion, are you not?
>
> **A:** That's correct.
>
> **Q:** And if you were shown convincing evidence that the facts upon which you based your opinion were erroneous, you would not hesitate to say so, would you not?
>
> **A:** No, I would not.[14]

---

[14] Richard A. Givens, *Advocacy: The Art of Pleading a Cause* (1992) 153.

Note: By using this technique, the cross-examiner has the expert verify that her opinion is only as strong as the foundational facts upon which it is based.

New Facts

Another technique counsel will use to challenge the foundation of your opinion is to present you with new facts you were not aware of or did not consider. See the case of *E.I. Du Pont De Nemours & Co. v. Robinson*, 923 S.W. 2d 549, (Tex. 1995). In this case, the Texas Supreme Court found that a horticulture expert would not be permitted to testify in a Benlate case due to his failure to rule out alternative causes. The court stated:

> Dr. W. conducted no testing to exclude other possible causes of damage to the Robinsons' pecan orchard, even though he admitted in his deposition that many of the symptoms could be caused by something other than contaminated Benlate. For instance, Dr. W. stated in his deposition that any number of things, including root rot, could have caused chlorosis, a yellowing of the leaves, on the Robinsons' trees. An expert who is trying to find a cause of something should carefully consider alternative causes. Dr. W.'s failure to rule out other causes of the damage renders his opinion little more than speculation.

The way to prepare for types of questions regarding new facts is to thoroughly understand the other side's theory of the case. Once you understand their theory of the case, you can anticipate the additional facts that will be suggested to you.

> **Q:** Sir, let's assume that the plaintiff was HIV-positive, would that fact cause you to modify your opinion as to the plaintiff's life expectancy?

> _____

> **Q:** Now, sir, let's assume that the plaintiff was involved in a second automobile accident two months before you examined him, would that change your opinion as to the cause of the plaintiff's injury?

Sometimes you cannot anticipate the other side's theory of the case because they have surprise evidence that will be presented only at trial. A good example of this is a covert surveillance tape of a plaintiff in a personal injury case.

> **Q:** Now, Doctor, let's assume that the plaintiff is capable of chopping wood, raking leaves, lifting filled garbage cans, and playing badminton with his children. Would these facts, if true, alter your previously stated opinion that the plaintiff is totally and permanently disabled?

Turning the Expert

Counsel will frequently attempt during cross-examination to "turn," or get the expert witness to change her opinion. This is usually done incrementally and with the assistance of documents or exhibits. When done skillfully, the expert is hard-pressed not to alter her opinion.

Here is an example of a cross-examination of a tire failure expert who testified at length on direct examination that a tire plug did not cause the blowout.

Q: Is it your opinion that whoever repaired the tire that failed at the time of this accident with the string plug did so negligently?

A: No.

Q: Is string plug repair OK?

A: There's nothing wrong with the plug itself as long as the customer knows it's a temporary repair.

Q: Referring you to the corporate Product Service Bulletin, it says never use that type of plug, doesn't it?

A: It might. I would have to look at it again.

Q: Directing — Do you have that exhibit in front of you? Right here.

A: Is that it?

Q: Exhibit 56 A. Down where it says never use outside plug or aerosol-type inflation repairs. Always use both a plug to fill the injury and the inside patch to fill a repair.

A: Yes, that's what it says. They've taken — There's one step further — their procedure one step further than the RMA.

Q: So is it your understanding that the company actually intended that all repairs be done with a patch from the inside?

A: Can you read that to me?

Q: I can restate it to you. Is it your contention that the company intended that all repairs be done with a patch from the inside?

A: Correct.

Q: With that understanding, are you critical of the tire center in Carol Stream for having repaired a tire on October 15th, 1988 with a string plug?

A: If they had this in their hands at the time, then they were violating the company's request.

Q: In your opinion, was it reasonable that the corporate philosophy did not include tires and tire repairs as part of its certified auto service center program?

A: I don't know what the philosophy was on that, sir.

Q: Do you know anything about their certified service center program?

A: Just peripherally.

Q: Do you know whether it included tires or tire repairs in that program?

A: It's my current knowledge that it did not include.

Q: Do you have an understanding that corporate representatives went into the tire store in Carol Stream on a quarterly basis?

A: I understand that.

Q: Do you have an opinion as to whether those employees should have determined how tires were being repaired at the tire center in Carol Stream?

A: If I were one of those employees, I would have determined — I would have tried to have determined that.

Q: Thank you, sir.

Chapter 4 Trick Questions and Trial Tactics

Overview

Counsel will use many trick questions and various trial tactics in an attempt to damage your testimony during cross-examination. It is important that you anticipate this type of cross-examination. You should be prepared for questions concerning:

- your area of expertise
- yes and no answers
- professional discipline
- your personal life
- initial contact
- your file
- time line
- restating an answer
- lack of first-hand knowledge
- junk science
- other experts' opinions
- recognizing the opposition
- tools of the trade
- lack of a report
- being a professional witness
- being a cold, calculating scientist
- making other professional mistakes
- "did you know" particular information
- causation
- charts and summaries
- opinion for litigation only
- demonstrations
- report and calculations
- texts relied on
- learned treatises
- absurdity of an opinion
- prognosis
- last minute change of opinion
- finishing with a flourish

Area of Expertise

Expert witnesses should expect to be cross-examined about what their precise area of expertise is. Extreme caution should be exercised in attempting to expand that area of expertise to encompass the particular case at hand.

In this example, the expert, a chemist, attempted to portray himself as an expert on product labeling. He issued a report which concluded that the warnings on a lacquer seal container were adequate. Note how counsel chipped away at and eventually destroyed the chemist's alleged expertise in product labeling.

Q: Let me ask you this, Doctor, are you an expert in the scientifically-based tenets of message transmission?

A: That's a hard question because all I can say — I can't answer that with a yes or no because I don't know what the standards of the field are exactly. I know that I have never — I have never, on a negative side, I have never taken any courses in it or anything like that. But over the years I have been involved with many cases that required me to make judgments about it. I think I'm someone who writes well and is conversant with all types of writing: technical, creative, whatever. I think I can tell, have a good judgment about when somebody is making the points that they should be making. After teaching for — in fact, my first teaching job was in the City, Newark College of Engineering, and that was in 1960. So one of the things about teaching is communicating and trying to get your students to communicate and judging their ability to communicate.

That's a long-winded answer.

Q: Do you agree with Dr. M.'s statement that there is now a well-established body of knowledge in communication science pertaining to the analysis of product warnings?

A: I don't agree with it. And I doubt if it's — it's really — it's kind of a subjective, relative statement that he's made.

Q: You take no position on that statement?

A: I take no position. I haven't read his work.

Q: Do you agree or disagree or take no position with Dr. William M.'s statement, he's from Yale University, that over 1,000 empirical studies on persuasive communication are published each year in the scholarly literature?

A: That's a statement I have no way of knowing.

Q: Do you follow any of the scholarly literature on communications or product labeling?

A: No.

Q: Have you ever applied a research-based communication approach for determining the appropriateness of on-product warnings?

A: I would have to say no.

Q: Can you list for me three or four journals that are commonly read by those who are engaged in the profession of writing product labeling?

A: No.

Q: Can you name one of them?

A: No.

Q: Can you name for me any one of three or four of the leading textbooks that exist in the field of those who practice in the professional field of product labeling?

A: No.

Q: Do you know who D. Burlios is?

A: No.

Q: Do you know who L. Barker is?

A: No. He used to play Tarzan, I think, but I'm not sure.

Q: He could have.

A: He's one —

Q: He went on to be a great scholar in product labeling, but apparently you haven't read his work.

A: Lex Barker.

Q: Can you name anyone of the four or five classic articles in the literature and science of product labeling?

A: No.

Q: Do you think you have them in your file?

A: Do I have them in my file?

Q: Yes.

A: It is — there's some possibility of it. I do not — what I have is one or two collections of articles on product labeling. I couldn't say that I have it in my file.

Q: So you can't as you sit here now say whether you are conversant with the theories articulated by Dr. Friedman on the effect of adding symbols to written warning labels on human behavior and recall?

A: No.

Q: You can't say as you sit here whether you are conversant with either the article or the data contained within the article by Janes and Boyles entitled, "The Effects of Symbols on Warning Compliance"?

A: No.

Q: And as you sit here now you can't say whether you are familiar with the article or the data contained therein written by Carney and Slessen entitled, "Communication Effectiveness of Symbolic Signs with Different User Groups"?

A: No.

Q: Are you familiar with, and this will just be the fourth, because this is a classic, Doctor, I just want to know if you are familiar with it, Goldhaber and DeTurk, "Effects of Consumer's Familiarity with a Product on Attention to and Compliance with Warnings"?

A: No, but it sounds like a very good paper to write.

Q: Sounds like a good paper to read, too, if you are an expert in the field, don't you think?

A: Uh-huh. I am not somebody who is an expert in how to construct effective labels. I made no claims to that.

Q: Or how to determine the efficacy of a label?

A: Well, I have a body of experience which I consider to be good labels and bad labels.

Q: What you consider to be?

A: Yes. It's more empirical, but yes.

Q: It's more anecdotal?

A: Well, I am not someone — I have not taken any courses in it, and I don't — I just don't know what the actual state of the science is. It might be something like psychiatry, for example, in which there's a number of things that are considered to be science by the people who practice it, and by others it's not considered to be as reducible to science. That's all.

Q: Well, some nuclear physicists don't think chemistry is science either. They think it's alchemy.

A: Well, there's some mathematicians who, you know, that's just — doesn't mean a thing.

Q: There's certainly a large body of what we'll call social science data in this field, is there not?

A: You are right.

Q: You are not an expert in that body of literature?

A: No, I am not an expert in social science.

Q: And as you said, you are not an expert in designing an effective product label.

A: That's right.

Q: And you are not an expert in determining, through the literature or scientific standards or the social scientific standards of the field, the likely efficacy of a label, are you?

A: Can you repeat that, please?

No. I'd like to — can I say something?

Q: You can say anything you want, Doctor.

A: I am not convinced of the reliability of this type of research.

Q: Doctor, have you ever studied the research?

A: I've read — my contact with it is in expert reports. Some of the material, some of it to me are — are not — do not seem to be practical.

Q: Some of it?

A: Yes.

Q: Doctor, you are not conversant with the body of literature, but you are ready to invalidate that field of science. Is that what you are saying to me?

A: I am not trying to invalidate it. I'm trying to say you've just detailed and recited a whole bunch of work in a field that I never said I was an expert in.

Q: OK.

A: And you are gilding this for effect, building up a whole bunch of "No, sirs," or whatever. But it doesn't mean that my judgment as somebody who's worked with hazardous materials over the years, someone who's also been involved in cases which involved labels, I've seen people say things like —

Q: You are back into slightly making a speech.

Don't worry about where I'm going. You answer the questions. Your lawyer will take care of where I'm going. Either you are qualified or not qualified.

A: Uh-huh.

I tend to be long-winded.

My point is that some things are not necessarily always best handled, particularly in areas of social science, best handled by some type of formalism that is set up for it. There should be some consideration given to experience in the field in terms of cases that I have been involved with and also my experience as a teacher. That's all.

Q: Doctor, are you familiar with that body of literature that experts in this field utilize to gauge the efficacy of on-product labeling?

A: No.

Q: Are you familiar with the methodologies that they utilize to gauge the efficacy of on-product labeling, what kinds of data they collect, how they work?

A: I have not studied that, no.

Q: Are you familiar with the government and regulatory standards that govern on-product labeling?

A: I have that in my file.

Q: Well, you are here today testifying to give us your opinion and the bases for it, correct?

A: Yes.

Q: As a scientist. So I am going to ask you a question. As you sit here now are you familiar with, for example, the health communication standards of OSHA?

A: I have seen them. I can't repeat them word for word.

Q: Can you tell me which of them are applicable in this particular instance?

A: I can't give you those numbers.

Q: Did you apply any of them in reaching your conclusions in your report? If so, which ones?

A: I can't do that.

Q: Can't do that?

A: No.

Q: Are you familiar with the SARA Title 3 standards for warnings?

A: I have looked through them. I am not familiar with them.

Q: What do the SARA Title 3 standards pertain to?

A: I couldn't tell you that right now.

Q: Have you looked at the CPC standards under the HFSA for adequacy of labeling?

A: I can't recall those.

Q: So as you sit here now can you say one way or the other whether they were considered in reaching your scientific conclusions in your report?

A: You are talking about the scientific conclusions about the labeling or the scientific conclusions about why the accident happened?

Q: Well, you have two, Doctor, so we are going to start with Number Two. That's where we are at right now. You express an opinion there about the label, correct?

A: Yes.

Q: OK. And previous to that, in "Conclusions," similar to a paper's conclusions, you there are basing — you say, "Based on the materials reviewed and my training and

experience as a scientist, my conclusions, to a reasonable degree of certainty are...."
You there mean scientific certainty, do you not, Doctor?

A: Yes.

Q: Now, what I'm asking you now is did you consider the standards expressed by the Consumer Product Safety Commission with respect to the Federal Hazardous Substances Act for, quote, labeling requirements, close quote, pertaining to, quote, hazardous substances, close quote?

A: I have in previous cases —

Q: That wasn't my question. In forming your opinion in this case, Number Two, the Number Two that's on page three of your report, were those standards considered in expressing this opinion? If so, which of those standards?

A: I cannot give you the standards that I used.

Q: Did you use them?

A: The way I worked in this case was I compared — I worked by analogy. I compared this label in terms of —

Q: Doctor, that's not my question.

A: Well —

Q: We'll get to your methodology in a minute. My question is different. I am still on the CPSC standards in reaching the conclusion.

A: I have read that material. I believe I assimilated that with regard to this type of label, but I — the way I worked with it was the completeness of this label, it seemed to answer all questions.

In fact, in reading your expert report by Mr. Kuzma, I couldn't see that there was any part of it — part of his objections that weren't met. In a previous — in a previous case there had been a situation — previous cases there had been labels that were much less adequate. This one was, in my mind, much superior to most of the labels that I have come across.

Q: See, here's my problem, Doctor. We'll end this portion and go back to the focused questions in a second. You keep saying, "in my mind." See, you are a scientist, but I think you'll agree with me, won't you, that not everything a scientist says is necessarily scientific, like Ponds and Fleishman. Isn't that right?

A: There's always that possibility, of course.

Q: In order to reach a scientific conclusion, a scientist must follow or purport to follow the scientific methodology. Isn't that right? It's a yes or no, Doctor.

A: What if somebody has — arrives — can arrive at conclusions without using — it's a question of how scientific is the scientific methodology in the field of labeling.

Q: But that, you told us, you don't know yourself.

A: I don't know that, no.

Q: You can't evaluate how scientific or not that is or how it would apply to your report or not, if in fact it is scientific.

A: That's not the approach I used.

Q: I understand. There are certain state standards in New Jersey governing the adequacy of labeling, on-product labeling. Are you familiar with those, the New Jersey standards?

A: No.

Q: So those would not have been considered in rendering your opinion in this case?

A: Yes.

Q: Are you familiar with any voluntary industry standards that have been promulgated either voluntarily by industry groups or by independent testing laboratories?

A: Well, I believe the paint — National Paint — I don't remember the exact name of it, but the industry group for paints, varnishes, etcetera, has standards. And I have had those and I have read those.

Q: In preparation for this report?

A: I have read them. And I had a case very similar to this before.

Q: That wasn't my question. Did you do it in preparation for this case?

A: No.

Q: Because it's not listed as one of the items, 1 through 13. The function of this is to — you understand, it's just like in your articles. It's to set forth the information that you are looking at, the database. It's not there. What does ANSI Standard Z 535.4 tell us, Doctor?

A: I can't tell you that.

Q: Do you even know what the subject matter of it is?

A: No.

Q: Have you read it?

A: If I did, I don't remember it as such.

Q: It is entitled, "Standards for Product Safety, Signs and Labels." Does it ring a bell?

A: I probably have it in that same file.

Q: Do you know whether you considered ANSI Standard Z 535.4 in formulating your opinion in this case?

A: I read certain material. I read certain material that had statements about the size of different warnings on a label, positioning, etcetera, etcetera. But I did not — I do not know these things by heart. I probably did read it.

Q: But you can't say —

A: I couldn't give you specifics on it. I can't say that I specifically did, but I read it. I looked through a number of things on labels for it. I can't tell you which ones.

Q: OK. Are you familiar with ASTM D-996?

A: I have read a lot of the ASTM literature. I don't know — I can't tell you just by the number of it.

Q: How about ASTM D-4326, are you familiar with that one?

A: I couldn't tell you. I don't memorize what the numbers are of the ones that I come across. Some of them I remember, some of them I don't.

Insisting on a "Yes" or a "No" Answer

Often the cross-examiner will attempt to restrict your answer to "yes" or "no." If you feel that you cannot answer the question with a yes or a no, state this and attempt to give your answer. While doing this, it is important to maintain your composure. It is equally important to not argue with the cross-examiner. If it seems reasonable that the question cannot be answered with a yes or a no, it is likely that the trial judge will not allow the examiner to insist on such an answer.[1]

In this case your reply to the question can be, "Sir, I cannot answer that question with a yes or no, would you like me to explain?" Here is an example of such an exchange:

> **Q:** Doctor, we're now looking at the next slide, 9D. And again, we see at a different magnification, we see scar tissue, do we not?
> In this deposition you have said you don't get asbestos bodies without asbestosis, isn't that right?
>
> **A:** Yes. And I said, that is what you just read.
>
> **Q:** In short, sir —
>
> **A:** Wait a minute. You're cutting me off, you don't give me a chance to finish my —
>
> > THE COURT: Doctor, just answer his questions, if you will. The cross-examiner has a right to call for a yes-or-no answer. If you can't answer yes or no, say so and then we'll see what happens. Try, in the first instance, just his questions. Thank you sir.
>
> **Q:** Sir, there's no question that is what you said, is there?
>
> **A:** Yes, it's what I said, but it's out of context.
>
> **Q:** This is what your testimony was in the Austin case, wasn't it?

---

[1] Roberto Aron et al., *Cross-Examination of Witnesses: The Litigator's Puzzle* (1989) 328.

A: With an explanation.

Q: All right.

Next question: "Every case of what, sir?"

Answer: "Where there has been a history of the inhalation of asbestos fibers, where there has been a history of exposure, when I have examined the lungs, this is what I have found, what I have just described."

You answered that under oath, didn't you, sir?

A: Yes, with an explanation. May I explain it?

Q: Doctor, you may point to the explanation in this passage if I haven't read it.

A: It's out of context.[2]

Professional Discipline

If you hold a professional license, you can expect to be questioned closely as to any disciplinary action taken against you by the applicable licensing authority. Do not hide past disciplinary actions from your retaining counsel. Opposing counsel can and usually will find out about any professional discipline you have been subjected to, as these are usually a part of the public record.

Q: Mr. Smith, you have been licensed as a professional engineer in this state since 1972, is that not correct?

A: Yes.

Q: Isn't it a fact that that license was suspended by the state licensing authority in 1988?

A: Yes it was.

Q: Your license was suspended for a period of six months, correct?

A: Yes, that is correct.

Q: And the reason given for this suspension by the board was "fraudulent and deceitful conduct?"

A: Yes, that was the reason stated.

Inquiries into Your Personal Life

An attorney may attempt to delve into areas of your personal life in an effort to humiliate or discredit you. Questions could be asked regarding topics such as alleged drug and

---

[2] A. Zabin, *Cross-Examination of Experts* (Massachusetts Academy of Trial Attorneys, 1996) 42-43.

alcohol abuse and past conduct. If you are subjected to questions such as these, stay calm. These questions are usually irrelevant and will not be permitted by the judge. Federal Rule of Evidence 611 expressly gives the judge authority to exercise control over the mode and order of interrogating witnesses so as "to protect the witnesses from harassment or undue embarrassment." The courts decide the extent of cross-examination allowed on a case-by-case basis. Following are some decisions regarding the scope of cross-examination.

Cross-examination limited

In the case of *Dixon v. Jacobson MFG Co.*, 637 A.2d 915 (N.J. Super A.D. 1994), the court limited the extent of cross-examination of a mechanical engineer in a snowblower product liability case. The court found that the proposed cross-examination about testimony in prior snowblower cases was intended to show the prior litigation and not inconsistent testimony.

Cross-examination permitted

In *Gasinowski v. Hose*, 897 p.2d 678 (Ariz. App. Div. 1 1994), the court permitted the cross-examination of an anesthesiologist about his subsequent suspension from the hospital.

In the case of *Winant v. Carras*, 617 N.Y.S. 2d 487 (A.D. 2 Dept. 1994), the court permitted counsel for the defense to cross-examine the plaintiff's expert on the issue of alleged drug addiction.

The courts have gone as far as permitting counsel to inspect the personnel files of a retired Los Angeles police officer who was testifying as an expert witness. See *Michael v. Gates*, 45 Cal.Rptr. 163 (Cal. App. 1995).

Counsel who retained you should object to questions about your personal life and you must give him time to do so before you offer a response. In the event that the judge does allow the question, simply answer it truthfully. An honest, direct reply can cause this type of questioning to backfire on the attorney using these tactics.

> **Q:** Isn't it a fact, Mr. Smith, that you are an alcoholic?
>
> **A:** Yes, sir, I am. But I haven't had a drink since I began AA 15 years ago.

Initial Contact

You can anticipate that you will be cross-examined about your initial contact in the case. You will be asked when and how you were called or contacted, by whom, what materials you were provided with, and on what issue your opinions were sought. Counsel pursues this line of questioning in an attempt to undermine your opinion by suggesting bias and a rush to judgment.

Cross-examination on the issue of initial contact usually goes as follows:

Q: When were you first consulted about this case?

A: June 14, 1994.

Q: Who contacted you?

A: Holt Bradley of the Kirstin law firm.

Q: Was that by telephone or mail?

A: I am not sure.

Q: What do your records indicate?

A: It was by phone.

Q: Do you have any notes regarding what information you received in that first phone conversation?

A: None other than the date.

Q: What were you asked to do at that time?

A: Review the records and opine on causation and standard of care.

Q: Do you have any recollection of the initial phone call — asking him what the facts were?

A: I never asked for the lawyers' view.

Q: Do you know how they came to find you?

A: No.

Q: What materials were you presented with initially?

A: [Expert lists the materials.]

Q: When you received the information, do you know in what order you read the information?

A: Probably as listed.

Q: Who did you receive all the documents from?

A: Holt Bradley.

Q: When did you first form an impression as to your thoughts in this case?

A: On the initial review.

Q: Did you review the plaintiff's expert information before forming your opinion?

A: I did.

Q: How did you put your opinion together? Was it after reviewing all of the information or did you do it kind of on a piece by piece basis?

A: Well, I take everything into consideration. The final products of my thoughts are contained in my letter of opinion.

Your File

When you are being deposed you can expect to be cross-examined about the contents of your file and what might be missing from it. Counsel does this in an attempt to question the foundation of your opinion. Here is an example of typical questions and replies on this subject:

Q: Have you brought with you the entire file concerning this case?

A: Yes.

Q: I would like to mark the file as Exhibit No. 1 and I would like to look at the file.

A: OK.

Q: I see a legal pad with some notations which take up three pages, is that correct? Are these your complete case notes?

A: Yes.

Q: So your entire file is before you right here in Exhibit No. 1, is that correct?

A: Yes.

Q: Have you taken anything out of your file?

A: No.

Q: Where are the reports you wrote in this case?

A: I didn't write any reports.

Q: Where did you obtain the documents in your file?

A: From Attorney Cohen.

Q: Did you receive any cover letters with any of these documents?

A: There were cover letters with a couple of them, yes.

Q: Where are those cover letters?

A: In the file.

Q: They are not in the file currently, where else would they be?

A: I may have some at home.

Q: Do you maintain a separate file for these cover letters at home?

A: No, I don't have a separate file. They may be on my desk at home.

Q: Do you agree to produce these cover letters?

A: Yes.

Q: Is there anything else missing from this "complete" file?

A: I don't think so.

Time Line

Counsel will sometimes seek to establish a time line of the forming of your opinion. This is done to discredit you. Counsel will seek to show that your opinion was formed so fast that it should not be believed. He may also attempt to suggest that you do not have adequate support staff to have completed your analysis in the time frame which you claim to have completed it.

Q: Mr. Smith, when were you retained by the plaintiff in this case?

A: November 15, 1996.

Q: That would be seventeen days ago?

A: Yes.

Q: Now, Mr. Smith, in only seventeen days, you were able to gather all the information that you needed, perform a proper analysis and form an opinion as to the cause of the accident which is the subject of this lawsuit, is that what you are saying?

A: Yes, I worked quickly because of the time demands that apply in this case.

Q: Wouldn't you have liked to have had more time?

A: Everyone always wants more time.

Q: I'm not asking you about everyone else, Mr. Smith, my question is would *you* have liked to have had more time?

A: Of course.

Q: You don't have a secretary, do you?

A: No, I do not.

Q: And you don't have any paid assistants?

A: That's correct.

Q: In fact, your consulting practice is based out of your home in Oklahoma, isn't it?

A: Yes, it is.

Q: Now earlier Mr. Smith, you testified as to the documents which you reviewed in forming your opinion, do you recall that?

A: Yes.

Q: And are these the documents which you reviewed?

A: Yes, they appear to be.

Q: Are you aware that they total 1,327 pages?

A: I don't know the exact number.

Q: You don't normally work this fast, sir, do you?

A: No.

Q: In fairness to the parties, sir, how much time would you like for a job like this one?

Restating an Answer

A common technique used by cross-examiners is to restate your answer. During the restatement, slight, subtle changes can be made by counsel. Do not allow her to do this unless the restatement is completely accurate.

Q: OK, Doctor, you previously testified that the plaintiff was malingering, did you not?

A: No, that's not what I said. What I had said was that the plaintiff's subjective complaints were not verified by the objective findings.

————————

Q: Now, Mr. Jones, you previously testified that you have had no formal training in this particular area, correct?

A: I have no recollection as to having testified like that.

————————

Q: As I understand it, what your testimony basically comes down to is that you say Dr. L. deviated from the standard of care because this lady ended up with a complication.

A: No, not at all. You didn't listen. I said that he deviated from the standard of care because she had a simple, semi-routine operation that resulted in a severe ureteral injury, one necessitating having to take a segment of the uterer out two days later and left an operating room and went into a ward where she had pain and somebody discovered that she was sick. That's what I said.[3]

————————

[3] *Seats v. Lowry*, 30 S.W.2D 558, 561 (Tenn. App. 1996).

Lack of First-Hand Knowledge

As an expert witness, you usually lack first hand knowledge of the facts that are at issue. This is one of the distinctions between you as an expert and a fact witness who may have made personal observations. You did not witness the crime, hear the damaging statements, or observe the effects of the injury on the plaintiff's daily life. Your opinion is based upon facts and investigations provided to you by others. Counsel may try to highlight this fact in an attempt to damage your credibility.[4]

Q: Now, Doctor, you have given your opinion that the plaintiff is totally and permanently disabled, have you not?

A: Yes.

Q: Well, isn't it a fact that since the plaintiff's accident you have only spent one hour with the plaintiff, to perform a physical examination?

A: That's correct.

Q: So you don't know if the plaintiff can mow his lawn?

A: In my opinion he could not do so.

Q: Yes, but you're not with him are you, Doctor? If he were able to mow his lawn, and did in fact do so, you wouldn't know it would you?

A: The answer to your hypothetical question is no.

Q: And you wouldn't know if he could play volleyball?

A: In my opinion he could not do so.

Q: And you wouldn't know if he could move a sofa?

A: In my opinion he could not do so.

Note: The expert kept calm and did not stray from his opinion.

Another example of this can be seen in the following cross-examination of an accident reconstruction expert witness.

Q: Mr. Smith, the automobile accident which is the subject of this complaint took place on August 8, 1995 in Boston, Massachusetts, correct?

A: Yes, it did.

Q: And at that time you were on vacation in the Greek islands, were you not?

A: Yes, I believe that I was.

---

[4] Michael E. Tigar, *Examining Witnesses* (1993) 245.

Q: Would a person who saw the accident or a person who at the time of the accident was 4,000 miles away in the Greek isles be in a better position to tell the jury what actually happened here, sir?

Junk Science

Counsel may attempt to attack your opinion as being based on junk science. This means that counsel will attempt to show that the methodology utilized in arriving at your opinion is not commonly accepted in the scientific community. Following are sixteen ways to counter an attack that your opinion is based upon junk science.

1. Be a knowledgeable professional.

2. Be meticulous with detail.

3. Be active in your field as well as an expert witness.

4. Have the opposing expert recognize you as an expert.

5. Show that you have testified to the same effect previously.

6. Show that your findings are consistent with studies by others.

7. Show your findings seldom lead to erroneous results.

8. Prove that new methods are positively related to prior methods.

9. Identify literature which establishes your approach.

10. Show prior admission of these same tests in other cases.

11. Relate animal tests to your results if possible.

12. Show why humans are not used in your experiments.

13. Relate your test to the same types of tests used by the opposition.

14. Show government approval of your methodology.

15. Establish that the scientific community relies on the same tests.

16. Use a back-up local expert to agree with your opinion.[5]

Note: See "The *Daubert* Challenge" section beginning on page 21 of this text for additional information.

---

[5] Ciresi, "Protecting Your Evidence Against 'Junk Science' Attacks," *Trial Magazine* (Nov. 1991) 38.

Other Experts' Opinions

You can anticipate that you will be cross-examined as to why your opinion differs from that of other experts in a particular case. The attorney may attempt to portray you and your opinion as strange and unusual. He will thus suggest that they are not worthy of belief.

Here is an example of falling into this trap and compounding the problem by explaining the answer in reply to an open-ended question.

> **Q:** Doctor, your opinion does not agree with that of Doctors Redfield, Hinds, or LaScalla, is that correct?
>
> **A:** That is correct.
>
> **Q:** Why is that, Doctor?
>
> **A:** I can't — I often have unique thoughts, and I can only speak for myself. I often see things that other people don't.
>
> **Q:** Is it usual for you to see theories and see things that other people don't see?
>
> **A:** To an extent, more so than other people. Yes. I mean, I don't want to beat my own chest, but…. There is no black magic here. I just have my mind, my knowledge, and my native intelligence.

Recognizing the Opposition

Opposing counsel will sometimes ask you to recognize the expertise of the expert she has retained. If you recognize the opposition's expertise, it will allow that expert to gain credibility. An example of how this may be done follows.

> **Q:** There could be various plausible theories as to the cause of this accident, could there not?
>
> **A:** Yes.
>
> **Q:** You are familiar with Doctor Johnna Smith, are you not?
>
> **A:** Yes, I am.
>
> **Q:** Doctor Smith has an excellent reputation in her field, correct?
>
> **A:** Yes, she does.

Failure to Use the Tools of the Trade

If you did not utilize a test or procedure which is commonly used in your field, you can expect to be questioned closely as to this failure. A line of questioning you could expect follows:

> **Q:** Doctor, are you familiar with the X test?
>
> **A:** Yes, I am.
>
> **Q:** Now the X test is a standard diagnostic test for injuries such as those alleged by the plaintiff, is it not?
>
> **A:** Yes, it is.
>
> **Q:** You didn't administer the X test to the plaintiff, did you?
>
> **A:** No, I did not.[6]

Lack of a Report

Frequently you will be testifying without having issued a written report. Counsel who retained you may have asked you not to issue a written report. This is done because a written report in many cases provides the opposition with further ammunition to use during cross-examination. You should anticipate being cross-examined about this issue. For example:

> **Q:** Have you written a report in this case?
>
> **A:** No.
>
> **Q:** Were you instructed not to write any reports?
>
> **A:** I wasn't instructed not to write a report.
>
> **Q:** Were you asked not to write a report, sir?
>
> **A:** Yes.
>
> **Q:** Who asked you and what did she or he ask?
>
> **A:** I was told by Attorney David that I did not need to submit a written report, that I should review the records and converse with her and we spoke on the phone.
>
> **Q:** Did you get a letter to that effect?
>
> **A:** Yes. It was in the cover letter.
>
> **Q:** May I see that letter please?

---

[6] Leonard Packel and Delores B. Spina, *Trial Advocacy: A Systematic Approach* (1984) 133.

Working as a Professional Witness

When an expert witness testifies frequently, she will be subject to cross-examination on the frequency of her testimony and for whom the testimony is offered. When an expert witness always testifies for the defense, counsel will often attempt to portray that witness as a hired gun or industry spokesman.

Here is an example of such a cross-examination.

Q: Sir, you've testified for Goodyear before, have you not?

A: Yes.

Q: Ten to twelve times?

A: Approximately.

Q: You've testified for Dunlop?

A: Yes.

Q: You've testified for Firestone?

A: Yes.

Q: You've testified for B.F. Goodrich?

A: I'm not — I may have. I'm not certain.

Q: You've testified for General?

A: Yes.

Q: You worked for General?

A: Correct.

Q: In the mid-1980s, 90 percent of your work was lawsuit-related, correct?

A: Was what, sir?

Q: Lawsuit-related.

A: Yes. Correct.

Q: You retired from General in 1987?

A: Yes.

Q: You've testified over four hundred times at deposition or trial?

A: Yes.

Q: And you've testified over one hundred times that a driver was to blame for loss of control of the vehicle after a tire blew out?

A: I'm not sure of that — to that number. I've testified to that before.

Q: Many, many times?

A: Some of the time, yes.

Q: OK. In fact, didn't you — Isn't it true, sir, that only one time have you not blamed a driver for a rollover following a blowout, and that's when the driver was going over one hundred miles an hour?

A: I think that's — I think I made that statement, yes.

Portrayal as a Cold, Calculating Scientist

Counsel may attempt to portray a technical expert as cold and unsympathetic. Expert witnesses should strive not to reinforce this portrayal with casual remarks.

Review this exchange, considering what impact this may have had on the jury in this death case.

Q: Sir, do you blame the driver for loss of control at the time of this accident?

A: I'd say he had to — his was a majority of the blame, yes.

Q: What's his name?

A: I don't know.

Q: You don't know the name of the person you're blaming for this accident?

A: His name is immaterial to me, sir. I'm not a legal person. I'm just a technical person.

Q: Is Mark Peterson immaterial to you, sir?

Have You Made Other Mistakes?

During cross-examination, you can anticipate counsel asking you if you have made mistakes in the past or other mistakes in a professional capacity. Answer the question honestly and briefly. If you are aware of mistakes you previously made, admit them and make counsel go on with his questioning.

Here is how the question may be presented. Note the honest but troubling reply:

Q: Have you ever made any mistakes in other inspections?

A: You seem to feel that we are not supposed to make any mistakes. If I say yes, I'm in trouble; if I say no, I'm a liar. You think we're supposed...of course we miss things from time to tome.

Q: So you have made mistakes in the inspections?

A: I defy anybody to say that they haven't.

"Did You Know?" Questions

Counsel will often preface a question with the phrases, "Did you know?" or "Are you aware?" The purpose of these types of questions is to highlight a fact before the jury. As always, answer truthfully. In the following example opposition counsel is attempting to have the witness recognize the authority of his expert.

Q: Did you know that Dr. John Smith is the world's leading expert in this field?

Causation

Experts are often called upon to give an opinion as to the cause of a particular occurrence or condition. When giving opinions on causation, you should be prepared to be asked on cross-examination about references to scientific, technical, or professional literature. This list should be prepared by you *before* you take the stand. You should also be prepared to respond to questions concerning other possible causes of the condition or conclusion.

Q: Doctor, you have just given an opinion that stress in the workplace aggravated the claimant's multiple sclerosis. Could you kindly tell me upon which scientific and professional literature this opinion is based?

A: Certainly, I based my opinion on the Kirshner Study, 42, *Archives Neurology* 859 (1985) and the Beganski Study, 17, *Annals of Neurology* 469 (1987).

Q: Doctor, isn't it a fact that multiple sclerosis is a disease of unknown cause?

A: Yes. But many diseases of unknown etiology can be aggravated.

Q: Isn't is a fact, Doctor, that persons with a family history of MS are eight times more likely to develop the disease?

A: Yes, it is.

Q: Now, isn't it a fact, Doctor, that you can't be certain as to whether or not the claimant's MS developed as a result of genetic factors?

A: Yes.

Q: And isn't there another school of thought in the medical community which states that MS may be caused by a virus?

A: That's correct.

Q: So you cannot be certain as to whether or not the plaintiff's MS was caused by a virus?

A: Correct.

Note: The expert maintained his opinion and was prepared with the necessary citations.

Charts and Summaries

The Federal Rules of Evidence[7] permit presentation of voluminous data through charts, summaries, and calculations. When this is done, the underlying information must be made available to the other parties in the case. If you have used charts and summaries during direct examination, you should be prepared to be cross-examined about the underlying information used to generate them.

Q: Mr. Smith, I see here on this chart, that you have charted the expected earnings of the plaintiff as both a paraplegic and as a healthy individual, is that correct?

A: Yes.

Q: And you have based this chart upon various documents that you have reviewed?

A: Yes, I have.

Q: You have no way of knowing whether the plaintiff would actually have achieved the earning levels that you list had he remained healthy?

A: Yes, that is correct, I have given his predicted earnings.

Q: And you based your estimate of the plaintiff's future earnings on the plaintiff's past earnings?

A: Yes.

Q: And on his education?

A: Yes.

Q: And his experience in his field?

A: Yes.

Q: Isn't it a fact, Doctor, that the plaintiff's past earnings were provided to you by way of a memo drafted to you by counsel for the plaintiff?

A: That is correct.

Q: You never reviewed the plaintiff's tax returns, did you?

A: No.

Q: Did you ask for them?

A: No.

Q: You have not independently verified the plaintiff's past earnings have you?

A: No.

---

[7] Federal Rules of Evidence, Rule 1006 (see Appendix C).

Q: You based his past earnings solely on what was represented to you?

A: Yes.

Q: You've never spoken in person with the plaintiff, have you?

A: No, I have not.

Q: You have no idea how he presents himself?

A: Yes, that's right.

Q: You certainly would have no idea how he presented himself before his accident?

A: That's right.

Opinion for Litigation Only

When your opinion, report, and testimony are obtained specifically for purposes of litigation, you can anticipate the following line of cross-examination. Once again, counsel is attempting to portray the expert witness as a hired gun.

Q: Do your opinions and conclusions in this case, Doctor, with respect to the causal relationship between Mr. Dukes' carpal tunnel syndrome and his job as a car inspector, grow naturally and directly out of research you have conducted in the area of carpal tunnel syndrome?

A: No.

Q: Do they grow out of scientific research you are or have been involved in as a doctor outside or independent of this or other litigation you may be involved in?

A: No.

Courtroom Demonstrations

Expert witnesses may be called upon to actually demonstrate or recreate the procedures followed in arriving at their conclusions and opinions. This kind of extemporaneous demonstration carries risks both for the expert witness and the counsel engaged in the cross-examination. This is a good opportunity for the expert witness to act as a teacher of the jury. It is the attorney's opportunity to get the expert to modify her opinion. If asked to perform a demonstration, try to appear fair and impartial before the jury.

Here is an example of this type of demonstration. Note how the expert taught the jury and how counsel got a small but significant modification in the expert's opinion.

Q: Doctor, can you show the jury — can you examine Mr. Holland?
And I'll move a chair out here, with the court's permission, your Honor, and —

A: Fine.

> THE COURT: Why not?

Q: — and show the jury his posterior drawer. Let me — let me get a chair. Can you do it while he's — you want him to do it sitting down?

A: Well, typically, we have him lying on a table so I don't — I could try it sitting down. Typically, what I do is have the patient lie on his back. I wouldn't suggest he get on that table.

Q: Can he do it on the floor?

A: Yes.

Q: All right.

Is that all right with the court, your Honor?

> THE COURT: It's his shirt.

A: Do you want to do it right here?

I'd like you to lie down on the floor. Face the other way because it's your right knee.

Q: Doctor, would you get as much drawer out of that knee as you think you can?

A: OK.

What I'd like to do is start on the normal side, OK?

Q: Yes.

A: OK.

Can everyone see? OK.

Tell me if I hurt you.

What I'm doing now is pulling the normal knee. This is the anterior drawer. What I do is just pull like that. And this would be posterior drawer. So this is the normal knee. And maybe there's a minimal amount of play. OK. This would be frontward. Anterior, posterior.

Now the other knee.

Q: Can you grade the left knee drawer?

A: I would call it fairly normal.

Q: OK.

A: OK.

So I want you to bring them both up.

[The plaintiff complies.]

A: And the first thing you want to do when you look for a posterior drawer is you want to see if it sags backwards.

So this bone here is called the tibial tuberosity. And you want to see if there's a sag. And I'm not seeing an obvious sag. So often with a posterior cruciate it will actually sag back. OK.

Tell me if I hurt you. You're too big.

OK.

Now, pulling his knee frontwards. And if you'd look at this, it's coming — this is — this is how one can confuse anterior and posterior. Anterior is this way. When I pull like this, it's does come — looks a little anteriorly. And when I push like this, this is posterior. And you can see there is a difference.

Let's show the other knee.

This one's stable. And when I go like this, there is a sag and there's no question there is a posterior drawer sign right here.

OK.

   THE COURT: That does it?

A: Thank you.

You OK?

   The Plaintiff: Yes. I'm OK.

Q: Thank you very much, Doctor.

You all right?

   The Plaintiff: Yes.

Q: Did you find a little more drawer today than you found in your exam?

A: Yeah, I would call this — this is — what I would call on the exam a one-plus, I might call now a two-plus. There's no question there's a posterior drawer sign.

Q: So now your opinion is that he has at least a two-plus drawer?

A: Yes.

Q: OK.

That's significant, isn't it?

A: I think it's significant.

Note: The witness' honesty in admitting a changed result probably had a favorable result on his credibility.

Reports and Calculations

Expert witnesses must be familiar with, and be able to explain to the fact finder, the technical terms contained in their reports and prior testimony. It is a serious mistake to assume that you will be able to overwhelm an attorney, who presumably is not a scientist, with terminology or jargon. If you cannot explain such terms, do not use them or rely on them.

Here is an example of what happened to an engineer who used some reliability data and was cross-examined closely about the formula:

Q: Let me get my copy of that report. Do you have that?

I believe before lunch we were talking about some reliability numbers that you used and calculated. Let's see if I can find them here. First of all, I put the number up on the board, 2.17 times 10 to the negative 3. Could you explain to the jury what the number means, as used in your report on page 1?

A: On page what?

Q: One, under the "Conclusions" section, where you say:

"The data indicates the average self-sealing fuel valve on these aircraft has a probability of failure of 2.17 times 10 to the negative 3 occurrences per flight hour."

A: Yes. That is a mathematical term for how reliable a valve is. In other words, what is the probability of failure.

Q: And then in the next sentence you say:

"This is a failure rate far in excess of the allowable 1 times 10 to the negative 9 or less for a critical system requiring an improbable failure category."

Correct?

A: Yes.

Q: Where does that 1 times 10 to the negative 9 come from?

A: That is an FAA definition of what's highly improbable. It's the goal that we design to get components and systems to meet.

Q: And is that the goal that if a breakaway fitting were going to be used that your opinion should be used?

A: Well, the FAA has said that it would probably accept 1 times 10 to the minus 6 or 1 times 10 to the minus 7 power if we could show that the engine had that same reliability.

Q: What do you think it ought to be, given your knowledge of breakaway fittings and your criticism of them?

A: I would agree that that failure mode is probably appropriate.

Q: Now, with respect to the 1 times 10 to the negative 9th, would you tell the jury how many years the Army UH-1 fleet would have to fly to prove the reliability for the value you think it ought to meet with no failures, as you define them?

A: You said to prove?

Q: Correct. In other words, how many years would the Army Huey helicopter fleet have to fly without having any problems with a valve in order to prove reliability to 1 times 10 to the negative 9?

A: That depends upon a lot of other factors.

Q: And you have those factors, do you not?

A: I have the factors for two years.

Q: Well, you know how many hours per year the Hueys fly, do you not?

A: Yes, I do.

Q: You know how big the fleet size is, don't you?

A: Yes.

Q: Can't you calculate for me how long that fleet would have to fly with no failures?

A: Well, that depends on how the valves are installed.

Q: Would it surprise you mathematically to reach the reliability of 1 times 10 to the negative 9? How many years would that fleet have to fly at the average monthly hours that it flies to prove the reliability that you say it ought to meet?

A: I didn't say it had to meet that.

Q: Well, let's just use that, and we will go back and talk about that a little further.

A: What is the basis for using the number?

Q: It comes out of your report, sir.

A: I said that was the design goal, but the FAA said it would accept whatever the reliability is of the engine.

Q: To meet this design goal that's set forth in your report, how many years would that fleet have to fly?

A: I don't know.

Q: Would it surprise you that it would have to fly 1,430 years with no failures to meet that level of reliability?

A: Could I see your calculations?

Q: Would that surprise you?

A: I'd like to see your calculations, please.

Q: Could you calculate it? Because we have got —

A: I'd like to know how you did it.

Q: How would you do it? Let's do it. You do it for the jury right now.

A: I don't have the data available right now to do that.

Textbooks and Articles Relied Upon

Sometimes a cross-examining attorney will ask you to specifically cite an article or text that you have relied upon to form your opinion. You must be prepared to provide her with the proper citation. Normally you will be required to bring them with you to your deposition.

> **Q:** Doctor, would you mind providing us with the citations of the articles which you relied upon which you claim support your opinion that cancer is caused by exposure to benzene vapors?
>
> **A:** I don't mind.
>
> **Q:** Do you have the articles with you in your file?
>
> **A:** No.
>
> **Q:** Are these the only documents you have removed from your file before today's hearing?

Learned Treatises

You can expect to be cross-examined with statements from "published treatises, periodicals or pamphlets" that were used in forming your opinion.[8] Additionally, counsel can use such publications to impeach your credibility if either you or another expert establishes that the publications are a "reliable authority."[9] Although portions of the publication may be read to the jury, they may not be physically submitted into evidence.[10] You should be thoroughly prepared to answer questions concerning any publications which you have relied upon in forming your opinion or which you recognize as reliable or authoritative. During cross-examination, counsel will attempt to impeach your credibility by highlighting apparent inconsistencies between your opinion and the content of the publications. Counsel will also attempt to impeach you by attempting to show that you disagree with recognized authority.[11] An example follows:

> **Q:** Doctor, you testified on direct that the plaintiff's manic depression was caused by the automobile accident that is the subject of this litigation, did you not?
>
> **A:** Yes, that is correct.
>
> **Q:** And in forming this opinion you relied, in part, on Dr. John Wilfong's text entitled *Psychosis and Trauma,* second edition?
>
> **A:** Yes, I did.

---

[8] Federal Rules of Evidence, Rule 803(18).
[9] Federal Rules of Evidence, Rule 803(18).
[10] Federal Rules of Evidence, Rule 803(18).
[11] Steven Lubet, *Modern Trial Advocacy: Analysis and Practice* (1993) 204.

Q: Referring to page 434 of that text, Dr. Wilfong writes as follows: "While the trauma of an automobile collision can occasionally trigger manic depressive symptoms, this is typically not the case. Usually the psychosis has a much deeper basis, and will not be excited by a single traumatic event in the patient's life, like an automobile accident."[12] Is that correct, Doctor?

A: That is what it says.

Many experts have been warned to not admit that any texts are authoritative for fear of being cross-examined about their contents. These experts are aware of the two general rules concerning the use of texts to impeach an expert witness during cross-examination.

Rule 1: An expert can be cross-examined about a text if she relied on the text, treatise, or journal to form her opinion.

Rule 2: Rule 803(18) of the Federal Rules of Evidence provides:

> (18) Learned treatises — To the extent called to the attention of any expert witness upon cross-examination or relied upon by him in direct examination, statements contained in published treatises, periodicals, or pamphlets on a subject of history, medicine, or other science or art, established as a reliable authority by the testimony or admission of the witness or by other expert testimony or by judicial notice. If admitted, the statements may be read into evidence but may not be received as exhibits.

The type of questioning you can anticipate follows:

Q: In reaching your opinion, did you rely upon any authority?

Q: Is your opinion in this case corroborated by authorities in the field of [the witness' specialization]?

Q: I have here a copy of...by...entitled.... The author is a recognized leader in his field, isn't he?

Q: Isn't it true that this book is currently used as an authoritative source in the field of [witness' specialization]?

Q: Have you read this book?

Q: Do you rely in part upon the teachings or views of [author of learned treatise] in reaching your opinion?

[Or, in lieu of the foregoing six questions,]

---

[12] Ronald L. Carlson, *Successful Techniques for Civil Trials* (1992) 345.

Q: I have here a copy of...by...on the subject of [witness' specialization]. Are you familiar with this book?

Q: Is it considered a standard authority in your field?

Q: In fact, it is an authority contained in the library of many other specialists in your field, isn't it?

Then [the attorney] proceed[s] as follows:

> [Reads the helpful passage to the witness and asks if he agrees; or hands him the book; points out the contradicting passage and has him read it.]

Q: Does this support your opinion or is it inconsistent with your opinion?[13]

Refusing to admit that a text is authoritative can also cause problems. When an expert witness refuses to admit that any text or article is authoritative, he may look foolish, biased, or even ignorant. For example, see the following cross-examination:

Q: Doctor, are there any books that you consider authoritative in the field of orthopedic surgery?

A: No.

Q: Are there any books that you consider authoritative in the field of orthopedic traumatic surgery?

A: No.

Q: Are there any books you consider authoritative in the field of traumatology?

A: Maybe you could clarify what you mean by authoritative. I'm having trouble with that.

Q: Are you familiar with the term authoritative?

A: That's why I'm asking you to clarify exactly what you mean by it.

Q: Are you familiar with the phrase whether individuals are considered authorities in your field, do you know that I mean if I ask you that?

A: In the sense that there's one thing that is sort of like the Golden Rule, I would say no to all those questions.

Q: If I ask you are there books that you consider authorities, not the definitive authority, but as an authority, are there books or texts that you consider an authority in the field of orthopedic surgery?

---

[13] Noenssens, *Scientific Evidence in Civil and Criminal Cases* (Foundation Press: 1995) 88-89.

A: I have to say no.

Q: Are there any books or texts that you consider an authority in the field of traumatology?

A: I have to say no to that also.

Q: Do you consider any book or texts an authority in the diagnosis of osteomyelitis?

A: I would say no.

Q: Do you consider any individuals as authorities in the field of the diagnosis of osteomyelitis?

A: Again, I would say no.

Q: Are there any books or texts that you consider to be authorities in the field of the treatment of osteomyelitis?

A: None that I know of.

Q: Are there any individuals that you consider authorities in the field of treatment of osteomyelitis?

A: No.

Q: Are there any books or texts that you rely upon in the diagnosis of osteomyclitis?

A: None specifically, I think I mentioned.

Q: Are there any individuals who you rely upon in the diagnosis of osteomyelitis?

A: Repeat that question.

Q: Are there any individuals that you rely upon in the diagnosis of osteomyelitis?

A: No.

Q: Are there any books, publications that you rely upon in the treatment of osteomyelitis?

A: No.

Q: Are you aware of other — of your peers in the field of traumatology referring to any texts as being authoritative in the field of osteomyelitis, that is the diagnosis of it and/or the treatment of it?

A: None that I'm aware of.

> *Note:* As you can see, failing to admit that texts are authoritative can be more damaging than conceding that they are authoritative.

Counsel will frequently attempt to get an expert witness to admit that statements in published treatises, periodicals, or pamphlets are reliable and authoritative. Once this is admitted under Federal Rule 803(18), counsel can cross-examine the expert about the article and read it into the record.

Here is a brief example of just such an exchange:

> **Q:** And, Doctor, are you familiar with the article entitled, "Oral Contraception: Past, Present, and Future Perspectives" by Daniel Mishell? And, again, this would be in the *International Journal of Fertility*, 1991. Are you familiar with that, sir?
>
> **A:** Yes.
>
> **Q:** Is that a reliable authority in the field as of 1991 on this issue?
>
> **A:** Yes.
>
> **Q:** And, Doctor, going right to the last page, to the conclusion, "Today 85% of prescriptions of [oral contraceptives] written in the United States specify formulations containing 30 to 35 mierograms of ethinyl estradiol, the lowest possible dose required to achieve optimal contraceptive [efficacy] with minimal risk of adverse effects. These new compounds do not appear to have any adverse cardiovascular effects and can be safely used by healthy nonsmoking, premenopausal women until age 45 or older."
>
> Did I read that correctly, sir?
>
> **A:** You did.
>
> **Q:** Do you agree with that?
>
> **A:** Yes.

In some jurisdictions, a simple admission by the expert witness that she recognizes a text as authoritative, regardless of whether it was relied upon, is sufficient to permit cross-examination with the use of the text. In other jurisdictions, the testimony by any expert that the text is authoritative is enough.

Here is an example where the expert witness readily admitted using an authoritative text:

> **Q:** Have you reviewed any books, treatises, or texts in connection with your work in this case?
>
> **A:** Yes.
>
> **Q:** What did you look at?
>
> **A:** Campbell's *Orthopaedics.*
>
> **Q:** Is that an authoritative text?
>
> **A:** Yes.
>
> **Q:** Why did you look at Campbell's?
>
> **A:** I think it's the quote, unquote, bible. It's, I think, the most authoritative general textbook in orthopedic surgery.
>
> **Q:** All right. What specifically were you looking for?

A: Just to re-refresh myself on posterior cruciate ligament tears.

Q: When did you look at that?

A: Yesterday.

Q: Did you look at anything before yesterday?

A: Well, I've read these things before.

Q: I know.

A: But I didn't do any specific reading on this case until yesterday.

Q: And which portion of Campbell's did you read?

A: It was — there's five volumes and it was the third volume. I don't remember exactly what page. But it was under the heading "Posterior Cruciate Ligament Tears."

Q: How many pages of Campbell's did you review yesterday?

A: I think it's all on one page or two.

Q: Also in your request to produce were any texts, journals, articles, treatises, etcetera that you read or relied on in this case?

A: Yeah. I think this pretty much sums up what I was reading, starting with this paragraph right here.

Q: OK. The Doctor indicated page 2368, a paragraph on the left-hand column, at the bottom.

Attacking Your Opinion as Absurd

Another common tactic that counsel will use is to use a *reductio ad absurdum* attack on your opinion. When doing this, counsel will first attempt to have you assert that the basis for your opinion is universal and applies at all times. He will then change the fact pattern to the absurd and ask if your opinion would remain the same. Consider the following example:

Q: Doctor, you testified that heart attacks are not caused or precipitated by work-related stress, is that correct?

A: Yes.

Q: So it is your testimony that heart attacks that immediately follow even an extremely stressful incident are not related to the incident?

A: Correct.

Q: So, Doctor, if I reached into my trial bag [lawyer leans forward] and pulled out a loaded 44-magnum and put it to your head and you had an immediate heart attack your testimony would be that that was a coincidence and was not related, is that what you are telling the fact finder?

A: That is what I am saying, sir.

Prognosis

Expert medical witnesses can expect to be cross-examined about their opinions as to the examinee's future medical care, disability, impairment, and employability. The medical witness should be careful not to leave his areas of expertise when prognosticating. This rule applies especially when asked what others might do in the future.

Here is an example of a cross-examination regarding the prognosis of the plaintiff:

Q: Doctor, fireman, policemen, you know, fire prevention and law enforcement, is a life or death thing, isn't that right?

A: Yes.

Q: You evaluate and treat firemen and policemen yourself, don't you?

A: Yes.

Q: And do you evaluate them and render opinions as to whether or not they can become a firefighter or a police officer or in fact can continue to be a firefighter or police officer, don't you?

A: Usually the latter. I'll see a police officer or a firefighter who's been injured and I will give an opinion whether they can work or not.

Q: Well, it's harder to get rid of one than it is to refuse employment to one medically, right?

A: I don't know if I can —

Q: In other words, if someone has an injury that's going to cause the city or county to have to retire an employee and pay him benefits, they're certainly not going to accept an employee for employment with the same disability, are they?
Do you understand my question?

A: I think I understand your question. You're asking me if someone has a disability prior to trying to become a police officer, are they going to accept them?

Q: Right.

A: I suppose not.

Q: It's unlikely, in your opinion, that Nick is medically able, given the present condition of his right knee, to become a firefighter, to be hired, true?

A: If he was having complaints and he does have this instability, I do not feel it would be appropriate for him to be a firefighter.

Q: Is the answer to my question yes, but it's unlikely, in your opinion?

A: Yes.

Q: And it's your opinion that Nick did not have this inability or disability prior to this accident, true?

A: That's true.

Q: OK. To sort of sum it up, he is medically — he was medically able to be a firefighter prior to this accident of October '92, true?

A: True.

Q: He is now medically unable to become a firefighter since the accident of October '92, true?

A: True.

Q: All as a result of this accident, true?

A: True.

Q: Now, based on what you found today, you'd agree this is a significant injury?

A: I would consider it a significant injury, yes.

Q: All right. And you agree that once you have a ligamentous injury of the knee, you're going to have degenerative changes much sooner than if you didn't have any injury to that knee, correct?

A: You're going to have acceleration of degenerative changes compared to the opposite knee.

Recross-Examination

Q: I am sorry, Doctor. I think I'm confused and I want to get a couple of things straight.

A: OK.

Q: Counsel asked you if there's a dispute about a tear, and then he asked you some questions about arthroscope, right?

A: Yes.

Q: OK. You examined the claimant on this floor. And based on your finding today, he has a significant instability, right?

A: He has what I would call about a two-plus instability, and I would call that significant.

Q: OK. So we're not — so he's got a tear, docsn't he?

A: I think there's a tear of some proportion.

Q: OK. All right. For the record, then, there is no dispute that he has a tear. He does have a tear, doesn't he?

A: Yes.

Q: OK. So we don't need to spend $4,000 to $6,000 and have him be off work for a month or two months to confirm what you have already testified is true, isn't that right?

A: Well, if you want to confirm a tear. But if you want to do a reconstruction, you need to do that still.

Q: Right. That's my next point.

A: OK.

Q: I'm sorry. I just do this in little steps.
There's a tear. He's got a significant tear. You don't need to do an arthroscope —
You're not recommending an arthroscope on this man right now, are you?

A: No, I'm not recommending any surgical procedure.

Q: OK. You don't need an arthroscope to grade the instability. You were able to do that right here in front of the jury, weren't you?

A: True.

Q: Now, given your findings of a significant injury and a certain tear of his PCL and given his size and weight, isn't it true, Doctor, that to a reasonable medical probability, this man is going to go on to develop post-traumatic osteoarthritis in his right knee?

A: To some degree, yes.

Q: OK. And to what degree depends on his size, yes?

A: It's a factor.

Q: His weight?

A: Yes.

Q: The activities he performs?

A: Yes.

Q: I digress for a moment. You're a baseball fan. Do you watch football?

A: Yes.

Q: And baseball? Do you know who Bo Jackson is?

A: Yes.

Q: Bo Jackson had a total hip.

A: Correct.

Q: Why?

A: Because he had death of his femoral head. He had a subluxation where it came out and the blood supply of the femoral head was interrupted and he actually lost the blood supply.

Q: And he felt so good he went out and started using it a lot, right?

A: Correct.

Q: He tried to get back in athletics.

A: Yes.

Q: And he wore it out, didn't he?

A: I don't know if he wore it out, but I don't think he used wise judgment to go back to professional baseball.

Q: OK. The point here is that activities that one performs on a day-do-day basis are going to have a great deal to do with whether or not they're going to be severely osteoarthritic at a young age or middle age, isn't that right?

A: That is a factor, activities, yes.

Reasonable Degree of Scientific Certainty

You may be prepared by your retaining counsel to state your opinion in a legally sufficient manner. For example, he may ask you to state that your opinion is based upon a "reasonable degree of scientific certainty." In a civil case, it is crucial for you to understand that this term means that it is more probable than not, i.e., at least a 51% certainty, that your opinion is true. You must understand this term in case you are questioned about its meaning during cross-examination.

> **Q:** Now, Doctor, on direct examination, you testified that the plaintiff's cancer was caused by exposure to Benzene, did you not?
>
> **A:** Yes, I did.
>
> **Q:** And you stated that your opinion was based upon a reasonable degree of medical certainty?
>
> **A:** That is correct.
>
> **Q:** Could you please tell us, Doctor, what you meant by a reasonable degree of medical certainty?
>
> **A:** By that I mean that it was more likely than not that the Benzene exposure resulted in the cancer.
>
> *Note:* An incorrect answer to the last question could result in the judge excluding your entire testimony.

Notes on Records

When you review records and make handwritten notes on the records, you can anticipate that you will be cross-examined on when you made the notes and what they mean. For example:

> **Q:** Did you make any notations on the records as you went through the case?
>
> **A:** Yes.
>
> **Q:** Are those notations reflected on this copy?
>
> **A:** Yes.
>
> **Q:** Please explain when you made each notation, what it says, and its significance.
>
> [Expert witness is forced to go on and explain each and every notation.]

Last Minute Changes of Opinion

An expert witness who changes her opinion regarding a critical fact in dispute should anticipate cross-examination on this issue. Counsel will attempt to portray this change as a desperate last minute action and as an attempt at ambushing the opposition.

Here is an example of a last minute change of opinion and the cross-examination that ensued:

> **Q:** Now, sir, you indicated during direct that you now believe the selector valve was in the left-hand position, correct?
>
> **A:** Yes.
>
> **Q:** But you were confident when you gave your deposition in this case in January that it was in the right position, were you not?
>
> **A:** When I looked at the records in September, I looked inside the aircraft, and it appeared to be an arrow on the forward side, which would indicate that the fuel selector valve was in the right-hand position.
>
> **Q:** When I deposed you on January 8, 1994, you told me it was in the right position, correct?
>
> **A:** That's correct.
>
> **Q:** And you didn't indicate you had any doubts about that, did you?
>
> **A:** No. Not from that observation, no.
>
> **Q:** And, in fact, at the deposition you brought out drawings and pictures and everything else and showed me why it was in that position, did you not?

A: Well, you asked me to explain how I arrived at that decision, and the difference here is there were marks on the valve; it was hard to determine where the arrow was pointing. There was no problem with the drawings or determining which way it was pointing as far as the drawings were concerned. It's a matter of looking and observing an aircraft that had burned.

Q: But you didn't indicate to me when I took your testimony that you had any doubts about that, did you?

A: No. You asked my opinion, and I told you at that time my opinion was, in September when I looked at that valve, that it was in the right-hand position.

Q: And it was your opinion on January 8, 1994, it was in the right position, correct?

A: That's the same time.

Q: No — September and January are the same time?

A: No. September is when I looked at it. You're talking about when you took my deposition.

Q: And you decided when — this morning — it's now in the left position?

A: No.

Q: Yesterday?

A: What I said is I examined my photographs. I had some very close-up photographs of the valve, and it appeared there was a small mark on the valve. It was the arrowhead that I showed the jury. And this morning I told Mr. Flores that I wanted to confirm that before I said anything about it. So this morning was the first opportunity I had to see the valve again.

Finishing with a Flourish

You, as an expert witness, should be aware of the fact that trial attorneys almost always try to finish their cross-examinations on a high note. They often accomplish this by pushing the expert until he says something that will likely upset or at least make an impact on the fact finder. This technique has been explained as follows:

> All manuals on cross examination rightly tell you to end strong. When cross-examining an expert, your ending must focus on bias, ineptitude, cupidity, greed, the conflict of expertises, the limitations of the particular expert's ken, the mutability of the expert's factual assumptions, or all of these. Your final questions should be a variation of the following:
>
> > **Q:** So, Doctor, if the jury finds the facts are what you assume them to be, you think they should agree with you, right?
> > **A:** Yes.

> **Q:** And if the jury finds the facts are different from what you assume them to be, they will probably disagree with you, right?
> **A:** Yes.
> **Q:** And, either way, it's their call, isn't it?[14]

Try to feel the rhythm of the attorney's questioning. Anticipate that finishing flourish and do not involuntarily provide the attorney with the damaging answer she is looking for.

Here is an example of how counsel pushed a safety expert until he got the memorable line he was looking for to finish on a high point:

> **Q:** Isn't it part of old factory history in New Hampshire that a lot of these old appliances and apparatus and machines are used for years and years on end?
>
> **A:** Yes, some machines are used, yes.
>
> **Q:** And if something is a serious hazard one day, assuming no changes, it's going to be a serious hazard with the same use and under the same conditions whether it's a week later, a month later, or five years later?
>
> **A:** It could be.
>
> **Q:** Thank you. And it's hard to tell just when that time bomb might go off and cause injury to someone, isn't it?
>
> **A:** We don't consider it a time bomb, but the injury is not predictable, perhaps.
>
> **Q:** You don't consider situations like this a time bomb?
>
> **A:** No.
>
> **Q:** Isn't that really part of the definition of serious violation, that it's substantially probable that someone is going to get killed or seriously injured?
>
> **A:** Only if they come in contact with it.
>
> **Q:** No further questions.

---

[14] Michael E. Tigar, *Examining Witnesses* (1993) 250.

Chapter 5 Cross-Examination of the Technical Expert

The best way to learn to excel during cross-examination is to practice. Unfortunately, expert witnesses are expected to be adept during cross-examination even early in their careers. Almost as effective as practice, however, is the review of other experts' techniques, mistakes, and experiences as set forth in actual cross-examination situations.

The following is an excerpt of a cross-examination of a technical expert in a product liability case. Headnotes have been added for the reader's convenience. A close review of this transcript will be extremely useful to all experts.

Cross-Examination

Attorney establishes background of expert

> **Q:** Sir, you've designed breakaway fittings into helicopters, haven't you?
>
> **A:** Yes, I have.

Counsel forces expert to answer the question

> **Q:** And is there anything in the federal regulations that would have precluded Cessna from attempting to certify crash-resistant technology in any of its aircraft?
>
> **A:** Well, you just said design these into systems into helicopters. We only do it on secondary fuel systems, not primary fuel systems. There needs to be a distinction about that.
>
> **Q:** Can you answer the question I just asked?
>
> **A:** Would you repeat?
>
> **Q:** Sure.
>
> **A:** You mean as I did in 1979?
>
> **Q:** Is there anything to have prohibited Cessna, in the federal regulations, from doing testing to attempt to certify the crash-resistant technology?
>
> **A:** No. Just as I did in 1979.
>
> **Q:** And the only time Cessna ever attempted to certify breakaway fittings or crash-resistant technology was with the T-41B, correct?
>
> **A:** I don't know what testing they did. I mean, I'm not aware of all the testing they may have done.

Q: Part of the work you've done, you've also designed special fuel tanks for military airplanes at Beech, isn't that correct?

A: Yes, I have.

Attorney establishes that safe tanks were available

Q: And, in fact, you designed a tank that you could shoot a 50-caliber machine gun through.

A: That's correct.

Q: And it would self-seal.

A: That's correct.

Q: With respect to your reliability report — and do you have that in front of you?

A: Yes.

Q: With respect to your report, you used supply data for your failures, didn't you?

A: You mean the number of failures?

Q: Correct. You used supply data, didn't you?

A: I used the data that is issued to order new valves to replace the ones that had failed in the field. Not the ones that are purchased but the ones that have failed.

Q: How many QDRs, in total, did you find for the helicopters in the Army?

A: I didn't ask for them. I have some, but I didn't ask for them specifically.

Q: Do you know for what time period those QDRs exist?

A: Most of them are about 1982 through '89.

Q: How many helicopters does the Army have this technology in?

A: There are about 2,941 helicopters, UH-1 models. That's all this report covers.

Q: Does the Army put the breakaway valves in other helicopters; for example, the Blackhawk?

A: Yes, they do.

Q: What other helicopters does the Army put these valves in?

A: The UH-60, and the -47. I'm familiar with those two.

Q: Any others that you're aware of?

A: There may be. They're the only ones I'm familiar with right now.

Counsel pushes expert on past product failures

Q: In the twenty-two years those valves have been used in Army helicopters, are you aware of any crashes that have resulted to Army helicopters as a result of the failure of breakaway fittings?

A: That's indicated in the QDRs, yes.

Q: How many?

A: Well, I only have a few. I have maybe ten or twelve that I asked for.

Q: How many crashes?

A: Well, you can't always tell if they all crash. Are you going to define failure by crash?

Q: My question is: Do you know whether any of the breakaway fittings failed and caused a crash?

A: Yes.

Q: How many?

A: I have one report of that.

Q: One report in twenty-two years?

A: No, that's not true.

Q: How many other crashes are you aware of in the last twenty-two years —

A: I'm aware —

Q: — that resulted from the failure of a breakaway fitting?

Expert inadvertently helps counsel by volunteering information

A: I'm aware there have been instances. They don't always crash and people are killed, but there are cases where the helicopters have to make emergency landings, auto-rotations.

Q: Are you aware of any other crashes in twenty-two years, other than the one?

A: I only have one QDR that says that. But that was not the basis of my report.

Counsel lays foundation for late calculation trap

Q: Now, how many flight hours are we looking at for all the Army's helicopters for twenty-two years?

A: I don't have that information. My report only covered the UH-1.

Q: And if you had gotten that information, you could make a calculation, couldn't you, in terms of reliability?

A: I concentrated on one helicopter and what happened with the valves in the helicopter, and the number of flight hours on that.

Q: And that's it?

A: Yeah. That was the subject of all this, yes.

Q: Now, what's your understanding with respect to how this crash-resistant technology has performed in preventing burn injuries and deaths in the helicopters?

A: It has significantly reduced the number of deaths in helicopter accidents, particularly in Vietnam.

Q: How about since Vietnam? How about when that Blackhawk crashed in Mogadishu recently? Was there a post-crash fire there?

A: No. But there was one in Germany — Panama six months ago. A UH-60 crashed there and everyone was killed by a post-crash fire. So the systems don't always work as they are designed.

Q: But do they work well?

A: Generally they work well.

Counsel introduces cost of human life into picture

Q: When you were at Beech designing fuel systems for airplanes, how did you account for the value of a human life in the cost analysis that you did in the design of airplanes?

A: I didn't get into that.

Q: That wasn't done in the design?

A: No. No, I said that wasn't my job. My job was to design the fuel system.

Q: And that wasn't part of that?

A: Pardon me?

Q: And using the — you didn't put a value on human life for purposes of your work in designing fuel systems?

A: Not me. I wouldn't do that.

Counsel forces witness to define key terms

Q: The definition that you used for failure and you told the jury about, where did you get that?

A: From the — There are a couple of reports that tell you how to calculate reliability. The definition is in that document.

Q: Do you know whether or not the FAA has a definition that it uses for failure?

A: I'm sure it does.

Q: What is the FAA definition of failure?

A: The definition the FAA uses for anything. In general, it's when the component fails to perform its intended function or if it creates some significant hazard.

Q: Anything else?

A: I'm sure there are other details. That's a pretty broad definition.

Q: May I approach the witness, your Honor?

THE COURT: Yes, sir.

Q: Mr. M., I'm going to hand you what has been marked as Plaintiff's Exhibit 23, which is the U.S. Department of Transportation *Glossary of Aeronautical Terms*. Have you seen that before?

A: Yes.

Q: Could you read to the jury what the definition of a failure is from that particular publication?

A: On page 29, the definition of a failure here is:

"The inability of an item to perform an expected or predicted function within previously specified limits. Failure should not been used in reporting broken, distorted, separated airframe structures, or components that were damaged as a result of loading imposed beyond design limitations."

Q: So, for example, if a mechanic happened to hit a breakaway fitting with a wrench and broke it, and it was replaced, would that be included within the definition of failure as you evaluate it for liability?

A: It could be. You'd have to look into the details for that. If it was done strictly as a maintenance item, I would say no.

Q: But, for example, your data that you used to do your reliability study would include such instances, because what you did is you took the data that showed how many of these valves were purchased.

A: No, I did not.

Q: What exactly was the data, then?

Expert witness corrects counsel

A: You may recall in my deposition you made that same mistake and I tried to clarify that. I did not use the number of valves that were purchased, I used the number of valves that were requested to replace the valves in the field that had failed. There's a big difference there.

Q: Just so I understand it now, if the helicopter mechanic, in changing one of the — in working around the helicopter happened to inadvertently hit it or caused damage to it and had to order a new one, that would show up in your reliability study, isn't that correct?

A: That's correct.

Q: Even though it had nothing to do with the operation of the helicopter.

A: That's true.

Q: And in terms of the data that you used — did all of the things that you called failures — were they incidents that caused the engine to stop?

A: No. They don't have to be. A failure does not actually have to cause the engine to stop. For example, leaking fuel in the cockpit, that doesn't cause the engine to stop, but certainly that's a hazard to the personnel nearby.

Q: And do you know, or is there any information available that would indicate what percent of these valves that you called failures were replaced because of something that occurred in the air, as opposed to damage that may have occurred on the ground, inadvertently?

Expert again volunteers information

A: No. There's no information to that effect. However, I did do a study in which I examined and said: Let's say 50 percent of all the failures were inadvertent. Let's say they were due to maintenance or something else. Now, it's highly unlikely that half of those failures would occur there, and still the failure rate was more than three times what is acceptable by the FAA.

Counsel furthers calculation strategy

Q: Now, let's talk about that for a minute, if we can. What failure rate did you come up with based on your study of the data you used? Wasn't it something like 2.17 times 10 to the negative 3? Was that the rate that you came up with, sir?

A: Well, to state that in a different way, that says that a valve would fail once every 460.59 hours.

Q: In your report, did you use the number that I put up there, 2.17 times?

A: Yes, I did. I was just trying to use something that was a little bit easier to work with.

Q: You also indicated in the report that your allowable limit was 1 times 10 to the negative 9.

A: No.

Q: You didn't?

Counsel lays foundation for lengthy attack on education and training

Q: Before we get back into the technical stuff, Mr. M., I'd like to clarify a couple of things about your background. I understand from your deposition that you graduated from high school in 1963.

A: Yes.

Q: And after you graduated from high school, you went to a school, the University of Missouri, Columbia?

A: Yes.

Q: And that was for a year-and-a-half.

A: Yes.

Q: What did you study while you were at the University of Missouri, Columbia?

A: Mechanical engineering.

Q: And why did you leave?

A: That was at the height of the Vietnam War, and we were going to be — at that particular time, they were drafting people into the military, so I went into the Air Force.

Q: And that's why you left school, to go into the Air Force?

A: Yes.

Q: Then you did six months in the reserves, is that correct?

A: That's correct.

Q: You went into the Air Force and you did six months' active duty?

A: That was training, aircraft maintenance school.

Q: OK. As an enlisted person?

A: Yes.

Q: And then after your six months in the Air Force, what did you do next?

A: I went back to college and attended Air Force reserve meetings and summer camps.

Q: And that college, I believe you told me at deposition, was Mississippi State University.

A: That's correct.

Q: And you spent a year there?

A: Yes.

Q: And you studied, I believe you said, aerospace engineering.

A: Aeronautical engineering.

Q: I'm sorry. Aeronautical. When you were there — and after you had been there a year, what did you do next?

A: I went to California for a summer job to work with Lockheed Missile and Space Corporation.

Q: And they hired you — Lookheed. Is that h-e-e-d at the end?

A: Yes.

Q: I believe you indicated during direct that you were hired by Lockheed as an engineer, is that correct?

A: That was a design draftsman.

Q: But did you indicate you were actually designing rockets when you were at Lockheed?

A: No. What I said was, I was designing the fuel system for a rocket. It was a rocket we used for installation of satellites into space.

Q: So you were designing the fuel system for a rocket, is that correct?

A: Yes.

Counsel implies expert was not qualified for past position

Q: And Lockheed hired you based on your education at the University of Missouri, Columbia, and your education at Mississippi State?

A: Yes.

Q: OK. Now, how long were you at Lockheed, approximately?

A: I think less than a year. Because of the build up in Vietnam, they activated a large number of Air Force reserve units, and my unit was activated at that time.

Q: So approximately a year?

A: Less than a year.

Q: OK. Let's see. And then you next got called up by the reserves and did a year-and-a-half active duty?

A: That's correct.

Q: And you were an enlisted man for about a year-and-a-half?

A: That's right.

Q: And, as I understand it, you did mechanical work with aircraft?

A: I was an aircraft mechanic for a period of time, then I became a crew chief, which means I was responsible for the maintenance on a particular aircraft.

Q: OK. So aircraft mechanic. Is that OK?

A: Yes.

Q: Now, when you got done with the Air Force, what did you do?

A: I went to work for Beech Aircraft in Wichita, Kansas.

Q: OK. And Beech hired you as a design engineer?

A: I don't know the exact terminology. I was a design draftsman working under an engineer at that particular time.

Q: Have you indicated in your resume that you worked at Beech as a design engineer since you went to work for Beech?

A: Yes. Not too long after I worked at Beech I received the title of design engineer.

Counsel attacks educational background

Q: And that was based on the college grade point average at Missouri and Mississippi State and your time in the Air Force as a mechanic that they decided to make you a design engineer?

A: No. Immediately when I came to Wichita I enrolled at Wichita State University. So I was attending classes at Wichita State University during the early period of time I was working at Beech Aircraft.

Q: So they made you a design engineer because you were in school for engineering.

A: No.

Q: Why did they make you a design engineer? What was the background that, to your understanding, Beech used in making the determination to make you a design engineer?

A: Well, you're now talking about different designations of hiring people in a company. There are different levels of design engineers, A and B grades. Also, sometime during my junior to senior year it looked like to them I was going to graduate within a short period of time. So I assume that all came together about the same time.

Q: Well, let's see. You started at Beech in what, 1960?

A: 1969.

Q: What year did you actually get your degree from Wichita State?

A: 1977.

Q: And that was a bachelor of science in mechanical engineering?

A: Yes.

Q: And you went at night while you were working for Beech?

A: Daytime and night.

Q: And Beech paid for that?

A: No. They paid a portion of it.

Q: OK. Now, after you graduated in 1977, you also did some graduate work?

A: Yes, I did.

Q: And that, again, was at Wichita State?

A: That's correct.

Counsel traps expert in not telling the truth

Q: OK. Now, going back to your earlier work. You did well in your classes at Mississippi State, is that correct?

A: I don't know exactly the grade point average.

Q: Did you tell us at deposition that you did well?

A: Yes.

Expert cannot retreat from his lie

Q: And did you do well in your classes at the University of Missouri, Columbia?

A: I don't know the grade point average. In other words, I don't know what the grades were. That's over thirty years ago.

Q: Are these all the colleges that you went to?

A: There was a summer class. I took a single class in Memphis, Tennessee, while I was working there during the summer.

Q: OK. What school was that?

A: Christian Brothers College.

Q: And you just took one course there?

A: I took a summer class there, yes.

Q: OK.

Judge, may I approach the witness?

THE COURT: Yes, sir.

Counsel stuns witness with transcript

Q: I'm handing you Plaintiff's Exhibit 225. Could you tell the jury what it is?

A: That appears to be a transcript of my grades.

Q: OK. First of all, grades are typically confidential with a school, aren't they?

A: Yes.

Q: Have you ever released those publicly?

A: No, I haven't.

Q: OK. So you have no idea how I would have gotten those grades?

A: No, I don't.

Q: OK.

Counsel explains he did nothing wrong

Q: Sir, I'm going to hand you now what is Plaintiff's Exhibit 226, which I'll represent to you is a certified copy of your application to become a professional engineer. And I'll ask you, sir, if your grades are attached to that information — which is your application to be a professional engineer.

A: Yes, looks like they are.

Q: So, having had the benefit of looking at that, do you now recall that you, in fact, submitted those to the Texas Licensing Bureau?

A: Yes, I did.

Q: Now, directing your attention to the classes that you took, and in particular your work at the University of Missouri, Columbia, in the first term, isn't it true that you flunked college algebra?

Expert now endures devastating questioning on his grades

A: Yes, I did.

Q: And you got a D in trigonometry?

A: Yes.

Q: And you got a D in American history?

A: Yes.

Q: And then you were placed on probation?

A: That's correct.

Q: And second semester, as well, it indicates you were on probation?

A: Yes. I had C's during the semester.

Q: And then in the summer you took the one course at Christian Brothers College, isn't that correct?

A: Yes, the one I got a B in.

Q: Correct. In econ. Then you went back to the University of Missouri, Columbia, for the first semester in 1964/65. Isn't it true that you flunked calculus?

A: Yes.

Q: And doesn't it indicate you were dismissed from school?

A: That's correct.

Q: And then in the second semester of 1964/65, you took a math analysis course at Christian Brothers College, didn't you?

A: Yes, I did.

Q: And you withdrew from that class in March of 1965, didn't you?

A: No. You'll notice it says "audit."

Q: Down below — I'm sorry. Go ahead.

A: It says "audited." That was a class I audited until I went into the Air Force. I withdrew at the point where I went into the Air Force.

Q: And then did you go back, sir, second semester of 1965/66 to Christian Brothers College in Memphis?

A: I'm sorry, I lost you. Where are you?

Q: Bottom of the left-hand column there, second semester, 1964/65.

A: OK.

Q: You went back to Christian Brothers College in Memphis, isn't that true?

A: Yes.

Q: And you withdrew from two of the classes you were taking that term, did you not?

A: That's right. I withdrew passing.

Q: Then in the fall of 1966/67 you went to Mississippi State, correct?

A: Yes.

Q: And you flunked calculus that first term?

A: That's correct.

Q: And you got a D in general physics?

A: Right.

Counsel toys with witness

Q: And then you got your first A in school that term, did you not —

A: Physical education.

Q: — in college. In bowling?

A: Yes.

Q: And spring semester, 1966/67, you got your second A in college, and that was in principles of insurance?

A: Yes.

Q: But the same semester you flunked the computer course you were taking?

A: I'm sorry?

Q: You flunked the course called IE 423, digital comp. fundamentals?

A: Yes. Yeah, that was a period of time when I found out my father had cancer.

Q: And you flunked that computer course?

A: Yes.

Q: And you flunked calculus?

A: Yes.

Q: And you got a D in physics?

A: Yes. That was a bad time.

Q: And you got a D in European literature?

A: Yes.

Counsel has completely destroyed testimony about education

Q: Now, let me ask you, Mr. M., have you ever been criticized by the FAA for violating any of the practices and procedures that pertain to DERs?

A: Early in my career I received one letter having to do with a procedure about witnessing a test. However, it was found that they were in mistake or in error, because there was a letter authorizing me to witness the test. That's the only time that a letter has ever been written, or a reprimand.

Q: But you do recall the FAA sending you a letter, and you would not disagree that that letter is in your public file, indicating that you had violated the practices and procedures of the FAA?

A: No. No, that's not true. After I found out that you pulled all my records from the FAA, I wrote a letter to the FAA to clear that up, because the people involved remember that I called them, and they found out they had authorized me to witness the test. I was to be absent from the test scene that particular day, so they authorized Mr. Ken Yeoman to witness the test. The test came and it went, he didn't witness the test so I went back and witnessed the test, originally. But the first letter was still on file.

The person who wrote the letter didn't know that. So a simple phone call cleared that up.

Error in expert's record corrected too late

Q: And that was after you found out I had gotten those records from the FAA?

A: It was a case where it wasn't worth anybody's time to follow up with such trivial information. But since you made an issue, I decided to go ahead and write the letter so it wouldn't happen again.

Q: But, February of 1985, you didn't think it was important whether or not that particular situation was clarified?

A: I did. I called immediately. I just said — if you will notice about the third paragraph, it says: "Please call if you wish to discuss this further." I called immediately, gave them the information, they checked it out, found out it was true, and the matter was closed.

Q: Do you have a copy of your FAA DER file with you?

A: Yes, because after you asked for it, the FAA contacted me and sent me the complete file.

Q: OK.

A: At least they sent me what they sent you.

Q: So you've had an opportunity to take a look at that?

A: Yes, I have.

Expert has never published anything

Q: OK. Let's see. Mr. M., you indicated in deposition in this case, and I believe in testimony here earlier today, that you've written some two hundred papers, is that correct?

A: I've written over two hundred reports involving certification of helicopters and airplanes.

Q: But you've never published anything?

A: Published? You mean to the public?

Q: Right.

A: No, these are all published internally to the FAA and to the client companies I work for.

Q: May I approach the witness, your Honor?

THE COURT: Yes, sir.

Counsel tries to prove expert lied to FAA

Q: I'm going to hand you, Mr. M., what is Plaintiff's Exhibit No. 28. First of all, would you tell the jury what that is? Did I say 228 or 28?

A: 228

Q: OK.

A: This is a Statement of Qualifications for an application to become a DER.

Q: And on the cover sheet you signed and indicated that all the information contained was true and accurate to the best of your belief?

A: Yes.

Expert evades counsel's attack

Q: Now, referring to page 2 of that exhibit, which is the resume that you submitted to the FAA to get that DER certification, you did not tell the FAA, did you, sir, that you had gone to the University of Missouri, Columbia?

A: No. What it is asking, or what I stated on here is I graduated from Wichita State University with a bachelor of science degree in mechanical engineering.

Q: But you didn't tell the FAA that you had gone to the University of Missouri at Columbia, did you, sir?

A: No, it wasn't necessary. They asked me specifically: What was you reeducation? What degree do you have, if you have a degree?

Q: And you didn't tell the FAA that you had gone to Christian Brothers College or Mississippi State University, did you?

A: I didn't graduate from those schools.

Q: So you didn't —

A: I only graduated from Wichita State University.

Counsel indicates other truthfulness problems of expert

Q: Let me ask you this, sir. You also indicated on the resume, master's of science, engineering management, degree work is 25 percent complete.

A: Yes.

Q: Isn't it true that when you put that down you had only taken two graduate courses?

A: I already had — that's true, two courses, but I had other credit hours that were applicable towards the degree.

Q: You had only taken two graduate courses by that point, had you not?

A: What is your definition of graduate courses? Any 500- or 600-level course is a graduate-level course.

Q: Looking at page 2 of your courses on the course schedules that we have, it indicates you were admitted to graduate school the spring of 1978, does it not?

A: You're on the second page?

Q: Correct.

A: Yes.

Q: And it indicates in the spring of 1978 you took a class in decision making and organizational behavior. Correct?

A: Right. For the master's program.

Q: I'm sorry?

A: For the master's program. Yes?

Q: I'm sorry. I didn't mean to keep cutting you off.

A: I'm sorry. We cut each other off. Would you repeat the question?

Q: And that particular copy or course work indicates that it was correct as of May 9, 1984, when you submitted that to Texas Licensing Bureau, isn't that true?

A: Well, actually I didn't submit this to them directly. That came from the school.

Q: Well, let me ask you this: As of May 9, 1984, had you taken any other graduate courses other than the two that are listed in this particular transcript?

A: The two graduate courses I took, I think which I got A's in, both of those were at the graduate level, specifically for management. Remember, this degree was for management of engineers, not technical aspects of engineering. But some of the other courses, 600- or 700-level courses could be or would be applicable to that degree.

Counsel shows expert's lack of scholarship

Q: Let me also ask you this while we are talking about your A's. Isn't it true that your first A at Wichita State was in basic public speaking?

A: My first?

Q: The first A that you got in a class was in public speaking?

A: Well, that was a required course.

Q: Did you get an A on that?

A: I haven't found it on here. Do you want me to look for it?

Q: It's spring semester, 1974.

A: Yes, I see it.

Q: And you also got an A in the spring of 1977 in a products liability course?

A: Yes.

Q: Now, going back to your resume, which is attached, or which is part of Exhibit 228. You told the FAA that you had eighteen hours of elective credits in the College of Aeronautical Engineering, including airflow theory and propulsion systems design theory. We can tell the aeronautical engineering courses based on the AE, can we not?

A: Not always, no.

Q: What courses, aeronautical engineering courses, are on here that aren't AE?

A: Well, the colleges, different colleges in engineering shared the courses. The only way I could tell is go back and get the college catalog from that year and determine that.

Counsel traps witness again

Q: But you were telling the FAA back in 1982 that you had eighteen hours of electives in airflow theory and propulsion systems design theory?

A: In propulsion systems, yes. My major turned out to be propulsion systems design. Mechanical engineering at Wichita State, since Wichita State is where most aircraft companies are located, that caters to people in the aircraft business, so that the courses are tailor-made for people who are in the aircraft industry.

Q: And what course related to propulsion, other than the propulsion course — your term — did you ever believe fell within this eighteen hours of electives? Maybe I should just ask that. Where do the eighteen hours come from? You tell me, sir.

A: You're asking me to go back about twenty years to figure this out. I could if I had a college catalog, which I did at the time I made out this application, but right now I couldn't tell you that.

Q: And you dropped that in subsequent resumes, did you not?

A: Dropped what?

Q: The indication that you had taken eighteen hours of electives in the College of Aeronautical Engineering.

A: I don't think it was significant.

Q: Well, you did drop it, sir?

A: Are you talking about the resumes I use today?

Q: Correct.

A: The resumes I use today are really based upon the experience of twenty-five years of designing airplanes. I didn't go back to 1970 to try to emphasize. It wasn't important. Once your license says a DER, or once you're licensed as a Registered Professional Engineer by the State of Texas, I don't need to do that.

Expert lied about publication

Q: Now, you also indicated in there that you had authored a book on the design of wing tip fuel tanks, published by Stanford University.

A: Yes. And I no longer list that, because the book did not get published. At the time I made this out it was planned to be published, but it never was.

Q: That was never published. So that was an error?

Expert cannot admit his mistake

A: No, that wasn't an error. The book — all right. Let's go into some details, then. The book was being edited by some book firm that was going to publish the book. But for some financial reason the book was not published. Now, that had nothing to do with my experience or what I did with the book or what I wrote in the book. That was a financial problem.

Q: But you told the FAA in that resume, quote, "I authored a book on design of wing tip fuel tanks, published by Stanford University"?

A: That was the publisher, and I was the author.

Q: Was it ever published?

A: No, it did not get published because of financial problems.

Q: But you told the FAA that you had published it.

A: What I'm saying is, the book — I wrote the book; it didn't get published.

Q: Why did you put on here, "Published by . . ."?

A: I'm telling you who the company is that's publishing it, that's all.

Q: Did they publish it?

A: It did not get into print, but they are the publishers. I understand the term publisher meaning the company that manufactures books. And what I'm saying is, that is the company that was going to publish the book.

Counsel exposes another truthfulness problem

Q: And when you sought your certification from the FAA to be a DER, you indicated to them you had been designing fuel systems and propulsion systems since you began at Beech back in 1969, isn't that correct?

A: Yes.

Q: And the only education you had to that point was your education at Mississippi State and the University of Missouri, Columbia, and the Christian Brothers College in Memphis, correct?

A: And what I had learned from working at Lockheed.

Q: But you were not a degreed engineer, were you, sir?

A: No. I was working under a degreed engineer there.

Q: And you were not a degreed engineer until 1978?

A: That is when I received a degree, that's correct.

Q: But Beech put you to work designing fuel systems for its King Air Aircraft?

A: I worked under a design engineer at that time, but that was my supervisor.

Counsel mentions other lawsuits

Q: Now, with respect to the reliability report that's at issue in this case, you actually did that for use in another lawsuit, did you not?

A: I was hired by a company to see if we could design an auxiliary fuel system for the Bell 212, 412 helicopters. At the same time there was a lawsuit going on against Cessna Airplane, and an attorney asked me to review that information. We decided to do a joint effort to see how the data would turn out, because I needed that kind of data to certify the Bell 212 fuel system.

Q: Cessna paid, in connection with that lawsuit, for that liability report?

A: Yes.

Q: And up to that point in time, to your knowledge, had there been any such reliability studies done?

A: I had not found any. I had looked for them, but I didn't find any.

Counsel attacks report and numbers used

Q: Let me get my copy of that report. Do you have that? I believe before lunch we were talking about some reliability numbers that you used and calculated. Let's see if I can find them here. First of all: I put the number up on the board, 2.17 times 10 to the negative 3. Could you explain to the jury what the number means, as used in your report on page 1?

A: On page what?

Q: One, under the "Conclusions" section, where you say: "The data indicates the average self-sealing fuel valve on these aircraft has a probability of failure of 2.17 times 10 to the negative 3 occurrences per flight hour."

Expert mistakenly believes counsel is unfamiliar with a term

A: Yes. That is a mathematical term for how reliable a valve is. In other words, what is the probability of failure.

Q: And then in the next sentence you say: "This is a failure rate far in excess of the allowable 1 times 10 to the negative 9 or less for a critical system requiring an improbable failure category." Correct?

A: Yes.

Q: Where does that 1 times 10 to the negative 9 come from?

A: That is an FAA definition of what's highly improbable. It's the goal that we design to get components and systems to meet.

Q: And is that the goal that if a breakaway fitting were going to be used that your opinion should be used?

A: Well, the FAA has said that it would probably accept 1 times 10 to the minus 6 or 1 times 10 to the minus 7 power if we could show that the engine had that same reliability.

Q: What do you think it ought to be, given your knowledge of breakaway fittings and your criticism of them?

A: I would agree that that failure mode is probably appropriate.

Counsel asks technical questions

Q: Now, with respect to the 1 times 10 to the negative 9, would you tell the jury how many years the Army UH-1 fleet would have to fly to prove the reliability for the value you think it ought to meet with no failures, as you define them?

A: You said to prove?

Q: Correct. In other words, how many years would the Army Huey helicopter fleet have to fly without having any problems with a valve in order to prove reliability to 1 times 10 to the negative 9?

A: That depends upon a lot of other factors.

Q: And you have those factors, do you not?

A: I have the factors for two years.

Q: Well, you know how many hours per year the Hueys fly, do you not?

A: Yes, I do.

Q: You know how big the fleet size is, don't you?

A: Yes.

Q: Could you calculate for me how long that fleet would have to fly with no failures?

A: Well, that depends on how the valves are installed.

Q: Would it surprise you mathematically to reach the reliability of 1 times 10 to the negative 9? How many years would that fleet have to fly at the average monthly hours that it flies to prove out the reliability that you say it ought to meet?

A: I didn't say it had to meet that.

Q: Well, let's just use that, and we will go back and talk about that a little further.

A: What is the basis for using the number?

Q: It comes out of your report, sir.

A: I said that was the design goal, but the FAA said it would accept whatever the reliability is of the engine.

Q: To meet this design goal that's set forth in your report, how many years would that fleet have to fly?

A: I don't know.

Counsel traps expert and gets devastating information

Q: Would it surprise you that it would have to fly 1,430 years with no failures to meet that level of reliability?

A: Could I see your calculations?

Q: Would that surprise you?

Expert desperately seeks help

A: I'd like to see your calculations, please.

Q: Could you calculate it? Because we have got —

A: I'd like to know how you did it.

Q: How would you do it? Let's do it. You do it for the jury right now.

A: I don't have the data available right now to do that.

Q: What data do you need sir.?

Mr. M., you've had an opportunity to look at the formulae I gave you during the break. Having had an opportunity to look at that, do you now have an understanding as to how one would calculate the number of years that it would take for the Huey helicopter fleet to fly with no failures before it would meet the design call of 1 times 10 to the negative 9?

A: Yes.

Q: And would you tell the jury how many years that would take?

A: First of all, you've done that incorrectly. Your math is not correct, in that the way you've done it, that the information you must have received on this talks about events that are not in hours.

Q: I'm sorry? Excuse me?

A: And you've mixed units with hours, which is not appropriate. So that method is not correct. But what I did say was it was 1 times 10 to the minus 6 power is what the FAA would accept, and that comes out to be being 1.42 years, which is a very reasonable number.

141

Q: Did you calculate it for 1 times 10 to the negative 9, which is the design goal in your report?

A: What I'm saying, the way you calculated it, this is not right.

Expert avoids performing calculations

Q: Would you calculate it right for me, given the thought you used to get the 1.4 years for the 1 times 10 to the negative 6?

A: Don't have enough information to do that. What I'm saying is, you can't do that without knowing something about the fleet size, the number of units, number of units on board each helicopter.

Q: Well, you've made certain assumptions to make that calculation for 1.42 years, have you not, that you just shared with us, with the jury?

A: No. I just followed your method. What I'm saying, that's not a valid thought. If you were going to do it that way, that is not a valid method.

Q: Why isn't it valid?

A: Because you're mixing events with hours, and events and hours cannot be mixed, the units are not correct.

Q: What events are we mixing incorrectly?

A: An event would be when one frangible fitting would fail.

Q: But what you're trying to figure out is how many years you'd have to go without that happening?

A: That's right. And you can't do it this way.

Q: And why not?

A: What I just said, that you have mixed these units, events in units with hours. That's not a proper way of doing this.

Q: But you also told me, did you not, that to reach the level of reliability of 1 times 10 to the negative 6 that it would take 1.42 years for the entire fleet?

A: I said — that's the number of hours if you were going to do it along those lines, but I don't agree that is a valid way of doing it.

Q: Well, doing it that way, sir, how many years would it take to reach the design goal of 1 times 10 to the negative 9?

A: I wouldn't do it that way.

Q: It's in your report, sir.

A: No, my report didn't say that at all. You're misquoting it.

Q: Would you read for the jury, please, the last sentence on your conclusions of page 1?

A: What my report is doing is figuring out failure rates, and you're mixing information that's not appropriate. That's not what this report did at all.

Q: Would you read to the jury what it said, sir?

A: Yes. Yes, I will be glad to.

Q: Last sentence under "Conclusions."

A: On page 1 under Section 3?

Q: Correct.

A: Titled "Conclusions." It says: "This is a failure rates far in excess of the allowable 1 times 10 to the minus 3 or less for a critical system requiring improbable failure category."

Q: Now, you're saying today that that is 1 times 10 to the negative 3? At your deposition, sir, didn't you say that was 1 times 10 to the negative 9 in your report?

A: You'll recall in my deposition I said the FAA would accept 1 times 10 to the minus 6 or 7, whatever the engine is equal to, and I said 1 times 10 to the minus 9 was the goal.

Q: And that last sentence, that's 1 times 10 to the negative 9 in your report, correct?

A: Yes.

Q: Now, you've told the jury, as I understand it, that based on your analysis of the supply data, you would expect a valve failure once every 460 hours of operation. Is that correct?

A: If you had a single valve in a critical application.

Q: And would you explain to the jury the method you used to calculate that failure rate? You took the supply data and what did you do with it?

A: It wasn't the supply data. Remember we talked about that?

Q: The purchase data.

A: It's not the purchase data, either.

Q: It's how many parts went out to people?

Expert corrects counsel

A: It's how many parts failed. Excuse me. It's how many parts failed in the field.

Q: Every one of those parts failed?

A: Parts are being replaced all right, and they are being replaced for a particular reason, probably because they are leaking or they have closed off and shut off the fuel supply.

Expert doesn't know answer

Q: But you don't know why all those parts are replaced, do you, sir?

A: I have a list of them.

Q: You know why every valve that's in your data was replaced?

A: No. But if you throw in a safety factor, let's say 50 percent, it's still more than three times greater than what's acceptable.

Q: Let's go to your failure data. We will use your term —

A: All right.

Q: — so we can avoid quibbling about what it is. And you've got a bunch of part numbers at the end of your report, correct?

A: Yes. Those were — that's a photocopy of what the Army sent to me.

Q: Now, what is the method that you used to calculate failure rate?

A: What's the method?

Q: Correct.

A: I took the number of failures and divided by the number of flight hours.

Q: Now, what was the worst valve that you found in terms of the failure rate? Was 209-060-692-1 the worst one?

A: Would you give me the part number again, please?

Q: Sure. The one on the left, 209-060-692-1. Is that the worst one in terms of replacement?

A: That is at the bottom of the page A-2, that is correct.

Q: Yes.

A: Yes.

Again, expert does not know answer

Q: And do you know where that particular part is located?

A: No. Some of these parts are in the fuel system, some in the oil system. The oil system could be just as critical as the fuel system.

Q: Do you know whether that particular part is in a location where it's frequently stepped on by mechanics that service the helicopter?

A: No. I assume if it occurred a few times they would eventually correct that problem, since the helicopter has been out there for twenty-five years.

Q: Well, using your method of calculation for failure rate, let's just do if for this one valve, which is the worst one.

And if I understand your method, what we do is we take the 34.03 times 12 for twelve months. Correct?

A: Yes.

Q: And then we divide that, if I am reading your formula right — let's see. We divide that by 699,180 — correct?

A: Yes.

Q: Could you calculate that out for me?

Expert forced to calculate on stand

A: OK.

Q: What is that?

A: That is .0015835.

Q: Thirty-five. Now, if I want to do that in 5.8 times 10 to the negative something, what is that?

A: That would be 5.835 times 10 to the minus 4.

Q: OK. Now, how does that compare to the rate you gave the jury, which is the 2.17 times 10 to the negative 3? Is that worse or better?

A: It's a little bit better.

Q: Can you explain to the jury how it is that the worst valve out of all the ones we looked at has a better reliability figure that the number you gave the jury?

A: Yes.

Q: Tell them why that is.

A: Because there are a number of helicopters out there that have partial systems installed, and others have total systems installed. In other words, some of the helicopters would have fewer valves than other helicopters. So, what I did was take a sampling of the whole group, or whole family of frangible fittings.

Q: What you, in effect, did, sir, did you not, is add up the failure rates?

A: I wouldn't say I added them.

Q: Well, you've told this jury there is a probability that a valve will fail once every 460 hours of flight?

A: Yes.

Q: But wouldn't you agree that the worst valve, based on this data, isn't going to fail that often?

A: Yeah. But you have a family of valves here of different designs so you have to survey the whole group. It's not appropriate to look at only one.

Q: But talking — I'm sorry?

A: Because in 1971 you wouldn't know which one was the good valve or the bad valve.

Q: But we are looking at the worst here, are we not?

A: You're looking at a number that's worst in this particular case, yes.

Q: And can you tell the jury, based on looking at this one valve — which is the worst one — what the failure would be in terms of one out of so many hours? For just this valve.

A: Well, that itself is — just a minute and I'll tell you. Your question was what is the failure rate?

Q: In hours, one every so many hours of flight time.

A: That number would be every 1,715 hours.

> THE COURT: 715?

Q: 1,750?

A: Fifteen. 1715.

Q: I'm sorry. Thank you, Judge. Judge, may I approach the witness, briefly?

> THE COURT: If you are going to hand him a document, that would be all right.

Q: I'm going to hand you Plaintiffs' Exhibit No. 227.

> THE COURT: I just don't want you to try to hit him, the way things are going.

A: Thank you.

Q: Is that the letter, sir, from your DER file we were talking about?

A: Yes, it is.

Q: And Exhibit No. 224 is a copy of your resume?

A: Yes. Judge, I'd like to pass Plaintiff's Exhibit 226, which is the application from the professional engineering license, the resume, as well as the letter that we referenced.

> THE COURT: Yes, sir.

Q: And just to clean up the charts here and put some stickers on them, the chart we have just been referencing I'm going to mark as Plaintiff's Exhibit 235, and the two pages of charts that relate to the background information — is the two — I'm going to mark as 236 and 237 for the record.

> THE COURT: All right. They will be marked. Do you wish them admitted?

Q: Yes, thank you, your Honor.

> THE COURT: They are admitted.

Q: Now, sir, how many engine failures does the Cessna T-210 experience in a given year of use?

Counsel tries a new tactic

A: I don't have that information.

Q: Are you familiar with *Aviation Safety*?

A: Yes, I am.

Q: Sir, with respect to the reliability rate that you have come up with, 2.17 times 10 to the negative 3 for breakaway fittings, do you have an opinion as to whether or not the breakaway fittings to be used should be more or less reliable than the engines that are used in the aircraft?

A: I'll tell you what the FAA has said, not necessarily my opinion. The FAA has said that if the reliability of the valve is the same as the engine — I should say valve system, not the valve itself, because if you put these valves in the reliability goes down tremendously —

> THE COURT: All right. Look, I mean his question is pretty simple. Can you relate the failure rates of the valves you're talking about to the failure rates of engines? You've said the FAA says it will accept a failure rate similar to the failure rates of engines.

A: That's correct.

> THE COURT: I see your point. So I guess that's why — the question is pretty simple under those circumstances. Do you have any information about the failure rate of, what is it, a Continental, Teledyne 1.0, whatever engine is in a Cessna T-210 aircraft? Do you have any information about the engine failure rates of those?

Q: Do you, sir?

A: Yes, I do — I don't have any exact numbers. No, I've asked for it, but unfortunately when I found out about the fact that you were going to ask questions about this the FAA has a lead time of two to three weeks, so I haven't received the information yet.

Q: Can I ask a couple of questions?

> THE COURT: Yes.

Counsel wants to use Aviation Safety *to cross-examine expert*

Q: Did you review the *Aviation Safety* article?

A: Yes, I did.

Q: And have you used *Aviation Safety* in the past for statistics in other lawsuits?

A: Never.

Q: Have you ever referred to *Aviation Safety* in testimony for information regarding the advantages or disadvantages of bladder cells?

A: I have my own opinions about that. I don't recall if I referred to them as an authoritative source. That's what you were asking me a minute ago about statistical data. That is not an authoritative source for statistical data.

Q: Have you ever referred to that magazine in testimony with respect to the issue of water contamination in fuel cells?

A: I have my own opinions about water contamination in fuel systems, where it comes from. It's possible the magazine may have agreed or disagreed, but that was not my source of information. I do not use that magazine as a source of authoritative information.

Counsel attempts to impeach witness with his prior testimony

Q: Do you subscribe to it?

A: No.

Q: Have you ever?

A: I may have.

Q: Do you recall being deposed in the case of *Leon v. Cessna* on April 22 and April 23 of 1986?

A: I was deposed in that case.

Q: Directing your attention — and I'll show you. Make sure I've go the right one. Directing your attention to page 310 of that transcript — it's right here. I'm sorry. This is so voluminous. Beginning on line 7 there's a question: "All right. The next page, 54 and —55."

A: Excuse me. Let me back up and read 309.

Q: Sure. Right here. Here. I'm sorry.

A: Let me see what the context is we're talking about.

Q: Sure. [Pause.] Have you had a chance to review that?

A: No, I'm still reading.

Q: I'm sorry.

A: OK. What was your question again?

Q: My question is, were you asked the question at line 7: "All right. The next page, 54 and 55, what is that?"

And did you give this answer? "I subscribe to the magazine called *Aviation Safety* and this article was in here about water contamination in fuel cells due to wrinkles. And I sent this to Mr. S. just as background information. One of the problems with bladder-type cells is that they get wrinkles in them and tend to trap water."

"Question: Is this a good example of what you were talking about yesterday in terms of disadvantages of the bladder cells?"

"Answer: Yes this is a distinct disadvantage, and as the wall thickness of the cell gets thicker, the problem gets worse."

Then the question is, just in completeness: "Is this article one of the articles that you relied upon in forming your opinions?"

"Answer: No."

Anything else you want to add?

A: No, you answered my question. I didn't have to say anything.

Counsel uses report to cross-examine expert

Q: I'm going to hand you what has been marked as Plaintiff's Exhibit No. 57, which is the T-41B report. And if you would, sir, would you read the summary on page 179 to the jury?

A: You know that there's about nine sections to this report and this isn't the end of the report?

Q: Would you read that, please, sir?

A: I'm just pointing out this is incomplete. I only have one section of the last page.

Q: Would you read that, sir?

A: Sure. Did you mean out loud?

Q: Please.

A: "The design and test effort reported herein has resulted in a crash-resistant fuel system fully compatible with the T-41B aircraft. The high-strength, flexible fuel cell, breakaway valves, breakaway attachments and structural modifications have considerably lessened danger of fire from fuel spillage in a survivable crash environment. The results of further testing to confirm the compatibility of the new crash-resistant fuel systems is reported in Section VII."

Q: Thank you. Would you tell the jury what the fuel quantity transmitter objects are in the wing?

A: What are they?

Q: What are they? These fuel quantity transmitter probes that are in the wing on Defendant's Exhibit J.

A: The purpose of the probe is to determine how much fuel is on board the aircraft. It's a fuel quantity gauge.

Q: Where were the probes found from the right wing of this plane?

A: One of the probes was found somewhere back along the wreckage — excuse me, back along the flight path.

Q: Do you know where the other one was found?

A: No.

Q: And is it your opinion that the one that was found somewhere back up along the wreckage, that it came out of that wing tank during flight?

A: Mostly came out of the right wing tank, yes. The left wing tank was totally intact, the right wing was ruptured.

Billing and fee questions

Q: Now, sir, Plaintiff's Exhibit No. 231, those are your bills in this case, is that correct?

A: Yes, they are.

Q: And those total, through January 31, 1994, approximately $33,793.33?

A: I don't see a total here.

Q: Do you have any reason to believe that's not an accurate amount?

A: You mean should I trust you? I will.

Q: Do you want to add them up?

A: No. If it's real significant, I will, but I'll take your word for it.

Q: How much are you going to charge Cessna for the additional work you've done since January 31?

A: My rate is $100 per hour.

Q: How much additional time have you put in since the end of January?

A: I don't know.

Q: More than $20,000 worth?

A: I don't — I don't want to guess or speculate. I don't really know. I don't think so.

Attack on last minute change of opinion

Q: Now, sir, you indicated during direct that you now believe the selector valve was in the left position, did you not?

A: When I looked at the records in September, I looked inside the aircraft, and it appeared to be an arrow on the forward side, which would indicate that the fuel selector valve was in the right-hand position.

Q: When I deposed you on January 8, 1994, you told me it was in the right position, correct?

A: That's correct.

Q: And you didn't indicate you had any doubts about that, did you?

A: No. Not from that observation, no.

Q: And, in fact, at the deposition you brought out drawings and pictures and everything else and showed me why it was in that position, did you not?

A: Well, you asked me to explain how I arrived at that decision, and the difference here is there were marks on the valve; it was hard to determine where the arrow was pointing. There was no problem with the drawings or determining which way it was pointing as far as the drawings were concerned. It was a matter of looking and observing an aircraft that had burned.

Q: But you didn't indicate to me when I took your testimony that you had any doubts about that, did you?

A: No. You asked my opinion, and I told you at that time my opinion was, in September when I looked at that valve, that it was in the right-hand position.

Q: And it was your opinion on January 8, 1994, it was in the right position, correct?

A: That's the same time.

Q: September and January are the same time?

A: No, September is when I looked at it. You're talking about when you took my deposition.

Q: And you decided when — this morning — it's now in the left position?

A: No.

Q: Yesterday?

A: What I said is I examined my photographs. I had some very close-up photographs of the valve, and it appeared there was a small mark on the valve. It was the arrowhead that I showed the jury. And this morning I told Mr. Flores that I wanted to confirm that before I said anything about it. So this morning was the first opportunity I had to see the valve again.

Q: Would you be critical of a manufacturer for using stainless steel fuel lines in the cabin of a single-engine airplane?

A: The use of stainless steel is somewhat restricted, but it may have special applications. There are lots of cases where stainless steel may be appropriate in the cabin of the aircraft for a particular reason.

Q: Does stainless steel have greater integrity than aluminum?

A: You'd have to define that. Integrity means a lot of different things. I explained how aluminum reacts in a crash. Stainless steel reacts differently. That's all.

Q: Do you have any data with you, sir, about whether the Army has ever experienced any problems with breakaway valves freezing in Alaska or in Antarctica?

A: I don't know if I have any data on that or not.

Q: You are aware that the Army operates its helicopters in cold environments?

A: Yes.

Counsel mentions other crashes again

Q: You've worked on other post-crash fire cases —

A: Yes.

Q: — involving the Cessna T-210?

A: Yes.

Q: And you are aware, in this case, that Mr. A., who testified yesterday, concedes that it's possible underbody fuel lines failed in this crash?

A: I'm not aware of that. I wasn't here.

Q: Do you agree that that is possible? Do you have any understanding, sir, of whether or not there was any fire in the cabin before the people who survived the fire got out of the airplane?

A: I know there was fire in the cabin, because the right-hand door was missing, and the fire came in from the right-hand side.

Q: And was that fire in there before the three that were in the plane had a chance to get out totally? In other words, Mr. Vincent Abeyta, Hal Kissinger, and Jo-Jo Rodarte.

A: I didn't look at that aspect of this case. My job in this case was to examine the fuel system and determine its crash-resistant characteristics.

Q: In connection with your work in the *Leon* case, that case also involved a Cessna T-210?

A: Yes, it did.

Q: And you had an opportunity to review testimony from other cases?

A: I may have. That was 1985 or '86, I guess.

Q: Do you have any recollection of having reviewed testimony of Harry Robertson from a case entitled *Smith v. Cessna*?

A: No.

Q: Do you have a recollection, as you sit here today, of whether or not in connection with your work on behalf of Cessna in the *Leon* case back in 1986 you reviewed any testimony from the case of *Smith and French v. Cessna*?

A: No, not specifically.

Counsel uses prior testimony to impeach witness

Q: What I'd like to do, sir, is — again referring back to your deposition in that case.

A: In which case? Smith?

Q: *Leon v. Cessna.*

A: All right.

Q: Directing your attention to page 61, line 8 — and that was trial testimony from the 1972 case of *Smith and French v. Cessna.*

"Answer: That is correct."

"Question: All right. When was it you were given the mission of determining whether it was practicable to put a frangible fitting or frangible fittings into the fuel system for the Cessna T-210?"

"You said when?"

"Yes, sir."

"Probably this year. And it was probably the January/February time frame."

"Question: What was the purpose for having you review the testimony, the testimony in *Smith and French v. Cessna*?"

"Answer: There was a witness for the plaintiff, and I believe his name was Robertson, who had testified about flexible hoses and fuel system components in a case in the past, and I believe the reason for sending it to me was to be familiar with what Mr. Robertson had to say about these components."

"Question: And did. . .."

There was an interruption. That was a question, "And did . . .."

All right. Then continuing the answer: "At that time, I believe they thought that maybe that lawyer, that particular lawyer may be involved in this case. That was just general information I had on the subject."

Were you asked those questions and did you give those answers?

A: According to that, I did.

Q: Do you remember now having reviewed the testimony of Mr. Robertson?

A: No.

Q: Do you have any recollection regarding Mr. Robertson's testimony regarding the availability of breakaway fittings in the early 1970s?

A: No.

Q: Do you have any recollection of having testified about that?

A: That I testified about what?

Q: Mr. Robertson's.

A: About what he said?

Q: Correct.

A: I may or may not have. That was eight or nine years ago. I haven't reviewed those documents for this case, though.

Counsel changes attack

Q: How many QDRs do you actually have for the Huey?

A: Do I actually have?

Q: That you actually have with you right now that shows there was some kind of failure for the breakaway valve for a Huey?

A: I have several.

Q: How many? Would you count them, please?

A: I'll be glad to count them. Do you want just the Army's or the FAA's, also?

Q: First let me ask: Were they marked as an exhibit? I thought the defense had those marked. If not, I would like to have them marked, but I don't want to have them marked again.

Is that them?

A: That's some of them, yes. That's not all of them.

Q: All right. What other ones do you have?

A: All of these. Those sheets you have.

Q: Defendant's Exhibit LL is what, again?

A: This is a number — this is a group of a number of Quality Deficiency Reports from the Army indicating failures of breakaway valves.

Q: How many different reports are there in Defendant's Exhibit LL?

A: Well, this isn't all of them. I have more here, but in LL there's a total of seven. And your exhibit has only seven.

Q: My exhibit? That's the exhibit that was marked between you and Mr. Del Hagen, correct?

A: Right, LL.

Q: And those are QDRs that you gathered in connection with your work on this case?

A: Yes. No, I'm sorry. Not in this case.

Q: On another case?

A: This is the data that supported, or actually was obtained at the same time the report originally was done in 1989, the '88-'89 timeframe. But since that time there are more.

Q: But at that time, in 1989, you only had seven reports of actual failures of these valves?

A: No. Remember, I said I didn't use QDRs at all, that they weren't used in my report or analysis whatsoever?

Q: That's because what you looked at was the data regarding product resupply?

A: No. I used the Army system. It wasn't my system.

Q: What were the QDRs?

A: I explained to you the QDRs are used to report unusual failure or multiple failures for documentation purposes. But the Army does not file one of these on every failure that occurs, so if you add these up you would come up with information that indicates the valve was better than it really was.

Q: Have you ever talked to the Army people at the center in Fort Rucker about what they use those for?

A: Yes. They referred me to ASCOM.

Q: Did they give you any information, in terms of the QDRs on the valves and how they compared to other components at Fort Rucker?

A: No. I said they referred me to St. Louis. Fort Rucker did not answer my question, they referred me to the St. Louis office....

Chapter 6 Cross-Examination of a Medical Witness

The career of an expert witness who is found not qualified to testify or is discredited in a case may be permanently marred or destroyed. In some cases this is what the cross-examining counsel is trying to accomplish. Thus, it is imperative that you gain experience from the review of expert witness transcripts.

Following are excerpts of the cross-examination of a medical witness who is a cardiologist. The case is workers' compensation involving a firefighter. Headnotes have been provided for the reader's convenience.

Preliminary Matters

By Mr. S.:

> **Q:** Hello, Doctor. My name's Mr. S. I represent the claimant. I'm going to be asking you some questions on cross-examination. I'm going to assume if you answer my question you understand my question. If you don't understand the question, will you tell me that you don't understand it before you answer it?
>
> **A:** Yes.
>
> **Q:** Thank you. Doctor, some of my questions will be asked in such a manner that they can be answered with a yes or a no. Would you, please, try and answer the question with a yes or a no and then let me know if you feel that there's additional explanation needed?
>
> **A:** Yes.
>
> **Q:** Thank you.

Counsel attacks expert's opinion directly

> **Q:** Doctor, having listened to your direct examination, I'm a little bit unclear about your opinion regarding fire fighting as a risk factor for developing heart disease. Is it your opinion, Doctor, that there's no such thing as firefighters' heart disease?
>
> **A:** There is no clinical entity that has been identified as specific to firefighters' heart disease, specific.
>
> **Q:** Is it your opinion, then, Doctor, that per se, work as a firefighter will not cause the development of coronary artery disease?
>
> > MS. T.: Objection.

A: No, that's not my opinion.

Q: OK. Would you explain?

A: There is a rare occurrence wherein, with no other risk factors, a firefighter comes down with coronary artery disease at an abnormal rate, and in those situations the relationship might be well established.

Q: OK. Well, Doctor, do you believe that the inhalation of smoke and fumes that one has as a firefighter causes coronary artery disease?

A: That has not been established. If you want me to guess, anybody is guessing. There are at least, at least, two publications that refute each other, one that demonstrates that that is so and one that demonstrates there's no relationship.

Counsel rephrases testimony to his advantage

Q: So, then, am I correct in understanding, Doctor, that it is your opinion, based on your understanding of medical literature, that there is no relationship between coronary artery disease and the inhalation of smoke and toxic fumes associated with fire fighting?

A: No. I believe what I said was that that has not been clinically established, so that one does not know for sure —

Q: Do you have an opinion, Doctor?

A: I — I base an opinion on fact. And until the clinical facts are shown to me, I don't know. When there are no other causes that I can establish for an individual firefighter who develops rampant coronary artery disease, then I find that there is a relationship, but there is no clinical basis for that. In other words, no good research, clinical research as has been done with the risk factors, as has been done with hyperlipidemia, etcetera.

Q: OK. Doctor, this is important, and I really need to understand it.

A: OK.

Q: And because I'm a layman, perhaps I don't understand what's meant by clinical factors.

A: Um-hum.

Counsel attempts to get expert to say the "magic words"

Q: So I'm going to ask in layman's terms: Doctor, do you believe that in fire fighting, the inhalation of smoke and toxic gases is either a risk factor or a causative factor in the development of cardiovascular disease in firefighters?

A: The inhalation of carbon monoxide has the potential, in one study, to precipitate that; to precipitate coronary artery disease. As I mentioned to you, that is not established, so I cannot give you a definite answer as to whether or not there is a relationship. That work is ongoing at the present time.

Counsel attempts to cast doubt on expertise of physician

Q: OK. I understand that you can't tell me whether there is a relationship. Does that mean that your opinion is that you don't know if there is a relationship between fire fighting and cardiovascular disease?

MS. T.: Objection.

Expert explains in too much detail

A: It's not that I don't know. It's that the clinical research, medicine has not established that there is a relationship. But I do find in certain situations that — that there is a relationship between the two, but there is no clinical evidence.

In other words, if we had 100 percent or even 50 percent of firefighters developing coronary artery disease as people who have the risk factors that I mentioned develop coronary artery disease, it would be fairly clear. That's just not the situation. There are good, controlled studies on both sides that refute and support that situation.

If you want me to guess, that's a different situation.

Counsel persists

Q: Well, Doctor, I'm asking for your opinion. You've been called as an expert in the field of cardiology. And the question remains, Doctor, in your opinion, does fire fighting and the exposures associated with fire fighting cause coronary artery disease?

MS. T.: Objection. This was asked and answered about three times already.

A: I must answer with this: I will take individual cases and review them. Some I will, and some I will not, find that the relationship exists.

Counsel gets expert to say, "It is possible"

Q: OK. So am I correct in understanding that you believe that it is possible for an individual to work as a firefighter and develop cardiovascular disease?

MS. T.: Objection.

A: It is possible for me to find the relationship. Whether or not that documentation can be established is quite questionable. I mean, I can establish risk factors associated with it, I cannot establish that fire fighting caused coronary artery disease, although, as I mentioned to you before, I find in favor of firefighters but I cannot establish it. It's just that the clinical evidence is not there yet. It might someday come. It might someday be refuted.

Counsel pursues expert's opinion

Q: Is it your opinion, Doctor, that fire fighting does not constitute a risk factor for developing coronary artery disease?

A: Fire fighting has not been established as one of the major risk factors by the groups that I mentioned before —

Q: OK.

A: — that is correct.

Q: Does fire fighting — does the inhalation of smoke and toxic fumes associated with fire fighting qualify as a risk factor for developing coronary artery disease?

A: That has not —

MS. T.: Objection.

A: That has not been established as such, as a major risk factor, as smoking. Cigarette smoking, for instance, does constitute a —a risk factor.

Counsel attempts to pin down expert

Q: Am I correct, then, in assuming that since you state that it has not been established as a risk factor, that in your opinion it is not a risk factor?

A: No, that's — that's not a fair assumption. I — all that I can tell you is that my mind is still open to that, is that — because it hasn't been established, it doesn't mean that I refute it. I don't know at this stage.

Counsel asks a compound question

Q: So, you have no opinion, your — you have no opinion as to whether inhalation of smoke and toxic fumes can cause coronary artery disease in firefighters?

MS. T.: Objection. I don't believe that's what he testified to.

A: I have an opinion as to smoking. Smoke can cause coronary artery disease. People who smoke are — do develop coronary artery disease.

Can firefighters develop coronary artery disease? Is that your question? I'm not sure what your —

Q: I'm trying to rephrase your testimony, Doctor, so that I can understand it in layperson's terms.

A: Um-hum.

Counsel attempts to get the expert to say he does not know

Q: And am I correct when I assume that it's your opinion that you don't know if the inhalation of smoke and toxic fumes associated with fire fighting causes coronary artery disease?

A: There is no established risk factor at the present time that constitutes what you just mentioned as a risk factor in coronary artery disease.

Q: OK. Let's talk about some of the risk factors that you mentioned before, Doctor, and how they apply to the claimant.

A: Um-hum.

Counsel sets up expert for causation question

Q: The claimant is of the male gender, correct?

A: That is correct.

Q: And he had some mild hypertension?

A: Mild, um-hum.

Q: OK. He was a smoker?

A: Yes, he was.

Q: He had family history of coronary artery disease?

A: No, I don't believe he had a family history of coronary artery disease.

Q: OK. He had elevated cholesterol?

A: Yes. He did —

Q: He had elevated —

A: — on some occasions, not on all.

Q: OK. And he had some elevated triglycerides?

A: That was a significant one, yes.

Q: OK. Now, Doctor, of those risk factors, which one caused his coronary artery disease?

A: A compilation of all of them.

Counsel attempts to blur causation and relationship

Q: Am I correct, then, in assuming, Doctor, that medical science has not been able to separate which of a variety of risk factors present in people with coronary artery disease causes the coronary artery disease?

A: As I mentioned before, the cause and effect is not there. The relationship is there. There is a subtle difference but an important difference.

Q: OK.

A: It's not like, you know, a bacteria causes pneumonia.

Q: I think I understand that, Doctor. And you had mentioned some other causes of heart disease, such as rheumatic heart disease, viral heart disease, and there was one other.

A: Congenital.

Q: Congenital heart disease.

A: Um-hum.

Q: Did the claimant have any of those?

A: Not to my knowledge.

Counsel leads up to the cause of the condition

Q: OK. So, you can't pinpoint any specific viral, or congenital, or rheumatic cause of his condition?

A: Yes. I hope I didn't imply that.

Q: Now, Doctor, there are other risk factors for developing heart disease as well, aren't there?

A: There possibly are one or two I might have missed.

Counsel pursues aggravation theory

Q: OK. And there are, certainly, risk factors for aggravating coronary artery disease, aren't there?

A: I'll — I'll listen to you as far as aggravation of such, yes.

Q: OK. And, in fact, stress is an aggravating factor for coronary artery disease, isn't it?

A: Acute stress is established as such.

Q: Well, Doctor, in fact, you've published articles stating that stress is an aggravating factor for coronary artery disease, haven't you?

A: Yes, acute stress.

Counsel asks for definition

Q: Doctor, what is acute stress?

A: Sudden stress that we all encounter. For instance, acute stress would be walking across the street, a Mack truck coming down on you, almost hitting you, heart beating fast, adrenaline rushing rampantly, blood pressure elevating, a headache occurring, as opposed to the chronic stresses that we all experience in everyday life.

Expert admits fire fighting is a stressful occupation

Q: OK. Would you agree with me, Doctor, that acute stress could be caused by going up to a burning building in the middle of a freezing night and not knowing if there are young children inside?

　　　MS. T.: Objection.

A: Yes.

Q: Would you agree with me that acute stress could be caused by being woken from your sleep in the middle of the night by an alarm bell and having to quickly throw on your clothes and jump in a moving truck?

A: Yes.

Q: So, you would agree with me, Doctor, that fire fighting probably qualifies as a stressful occupation?

A: I would agree.

Q: So in fact, then, the claimant had another risk factor for at least aggravating his coronary artery disease, and that would be the stress associated with acting as a firefighter, correct?

A: I never mentioned stress as a risk factor. If you want to rephrase your question, that would be fine. But stress, in and of itself, is not a risk factor nor did I mention it as a risk factor.

Q: I'm sorry if I misspoke, Doctor. I don't mean to state that you implied that stress, or imply that stress, is a cause. But, certainly, stress is an aggravating factor in a person that already suffers from coronary artery disease; wouldn't you agree?

A: No.

Q: You would not agree that stress aggravates underlying coronary artery disease?

A: If you read my article, that article stated that the stress from a heart attack killed the person, which is a little different from the progression of coronary artery disease.

Q: OK.

Counsel pushes expert to take a position

A: Acute stress is quite different. A heart attack is quite different from the progression of coronary artery disease.

Q: I see. So, it's your opinion, then, that stress has no — is not an aggravating factor for somebody with coronary artery disease?

MS. T.: Objection.

A: That has not been established.

Q: OK. So, when you have a patient that has coronary artery disease, do you tell them to keep living their stressful life?

A: That's a fair question. No, I — I try to take a lot of possible ingredients out of their life.

Q: Why is that?

A: Because of the potential of it occurring.

Expert's initial contact by counsel

Q: Doctor, let's change directions. Would you tell us about how you became involved in this case?

A: Yes. I believe Mr. J., Attorney J., called me and asked me to review the records of the claimant and to render an opinion as to whether or not I thought there was a relationship between his occupation and the — and his coronary artery disease.

Q: When did you receive this telephone call from Mr. J.?

A: Gee, I would only guess possibly a month or two ago.

Q: If you —

A: I'm — I'm not sure of the time.

Q: Do you have any notes to that effect?

A: No, I haven't.

Q: Any records of your conversation, your first initial conversation with him?

A: No, I do not.

Q: Well, when did you receive the materials from Mr. J.? He did provide you with materials, didn't he?

A: Yes. He did.

Q: He provided you with the records that you reviewed?

A: Yes.

Counsel shows expert did not ask for records or examine claimant

> **Q:** Did you undertake any individual research to obtain any other records?
>
> **A:** No, I did not.
>
> **Q:** And you did not examine the patient?
>
> **A:** That is correct.
>
> **Q:** So, you don't know —

Expert does not know if he had all the records

> **Q:** — if the records that you saw are the complete history and records of the medical care provided to the claimant?
>
> **A:** That is correct.
>
> **Q:** And any history that you may have had about the development of his disease and his job duties would come purely from what you reviewed from materials provided to you by Mr. J.?
>
> **A:** That is correct.

Counsel starts to show expert's poor memory

> **Q:** OK. Did Mr. J. send you the materials in the mail?
>
> **A:** I believe some came in the mail. Possibly some came by FedEx.
>
> **Q:** Where are the envelopes that they were transmitted with?
>
>> MS. T.: Objection.
>
> **Q:** Were they transmitted in envelopes?
>
> **A:** I would assume they were, but I would not swear by it.

Expert is not board certified

> **Q:** Doctor, are you board certified in cardiology?
>
> **A:** I am board eligible.
>
> **Q:** That means you can — you are eligible to take the boards but you haven't, correct?
>
> **A:** I have not, that's right.
>
> **Q:** OK. So the answer is, "No, I'm not board certified," correct?

Doctor refuses to admit he is not board certified

> **A:** I'm board eligible, that's correct.

Q: Well, the answer to my question was, Doctor, you are not board certified, correct?

MS. T.: Objection.

A: That's correct.

Counsel notes that expert's testimony may have been scripted

Q: Now, Doctor, prior to the deposition I noticed that you had prepared a written two-page list of questions. Can I see those, please? Doctor, I'm going to hand you what's been marked as Plaintiff's Exhibit 1 and ask you to take a look at it. Have you seen that before?

A: Yes, I have.

Q: Can you identify that, please, for the jury?

A: I wrote these questions as a — a prelude to Attorney J. questioning me.

Q: Did you write the — so, what is contained on those two pages, Doctor?

A: Questions. Questions about heart disease and firemen.

Q: Are those questions that you wanted Mr. J. to ask you?

A: It — they were questions that I thought would bring light to the jury as to why I — my opinion was what it was.

Q: OK. And you prepared that for Mr. J.?

A: That is correct.

Counsel points to poor memory of witness

Q: OK. Now, you've mentioned one telephone conversation at a time period that you don't exactly remember where Mr. J. asked you to review some records. When was your next contact with Mr. J. and — and what was the form of that contact?

A: I believe it was within the past week, asking me if I would give a deposition in this case. I'm not sure of the exact date.

Q: Again, do you have any notes?

A: No, I haven't.

Q: No records of your conversation?

A: That is correct.

Q: Now, after you reviewed the package, or packages, of materials that were sent to you by Mr. J., did you discuss your findings with him?

A: I don't recall if I discussed the findings. I —I sent him an opinion as to the — as to the findings.

Q: Well, you wrote a report, correct, Doctor?

A: That is correct.

Q: And I've seen a copy of that report, correct?

A: I believe you have.

Q: It is dated December 7, 1994?

A: That — that is consistent with when I sent it, yes.

Counsel points out last minute report

Q: So that was about two days ago you prepared a report for Mr. J., correct?

A: That is correct.

Q: OK. And how did you know to prepare that report?

A: He asked me to.

Q: How did he ask you?

Expert is unclear about details

Q: Did he ask you by telephone?

A: I would imagine by telephone.

Q: Well, did you have a discussion with him about the case at the time that he asked you to prepare the report?

A: I would imagine we did discuss it. I'm not — I'm not familiar with that conversation. I don't recall.

Q: You don't recall the substance of your conversation with Mr. J. that precipitated your preparing a report for him?

A: He asked me to send him a report, and I sent him that re— in fact, I faxed — no. I think I sent him the report, or I sent him the tape of the report.

Q: OK. And that was about two weeks ago, Doctor?

A: No. It was last — this past week.

Q: About a week ago?

    MS. T.: Objection.

A: Within the past week.

Counsel notes absurdity of testimony

Q: OK. So, you're telling this jury, Doctor, that you don't remember the substance of a telephone conversation that you had with Mr. J. one week ago about a case that you've just testified to this jury?

MS. T.: Objection.

A: That is correct.

Q: OK. What other conversations did you have with Mr. J.?

A: We had a conversation moments prior to this deposition.

Q: And what was the substance of that conversation?

A: Basically going over these questions that you just handed to me.

Q: OK. You reviewed the sheet that you had prepared for him?

A: That's correct.

Counsel attacks expert's prior work for counsel

Q: OK. Have you testified on behalf of Mr. J. or Mr. J.'s client in the past?

A: You mean the Attorney General's office?

Q: On other occasions.

A: Yes.

Q: OK. So far, Doctor, as I understand it, there are three conversations that you've had with Mr. J.: One was where he asked you to review some records, the second was where he asked you to prepare a report, and the third was the conversation that you had with him before this deposition. Is that correct?

A: To my recollection.

Q: OK. About how much time did you spend preparing for the report that you wrote?

A: Hours.

Q: How many?

A: Maybe five hours.

Q: You reviewed the medical records of the claimant for five hours?

A: Yes.

Q: OK. Do you have any reason to believe that the claimant was not a firefighter?

A: No, I have no reason to believe that.

Counsel asks about fees

Q: Doctor, are you paid on an hourly basis or by a flat fee for your report?

A: You know, in all honesty, I haven't submitted a fee and I haven't thought about it yet. Usually it's an hourly basis, but I haven't thought about it yet. It — it's been, relatively, a short period of time.

Q: OK. Now, Doctor, you testified that there were no clinical signs that the claimant's work as a firefighter either caused or accelerated his coronary artery disease, is that correct?

A: I believe I did state that. I'll — I'll correct that if — if I find that that's a misstatement. But I'll go along with what you just said.

Q: Well, as I — am I correctly rephrasing the —

A: I — I'm—

Q: — your testimony?

A: Well, I don't know what's in the records, if that's the exact statement, but I will accept that statement.

Q: Well, I'll — I'll rephrase the question, then, Doctor. Is it your belief that there were no clinical signs that the claimant's work as a firefighter accelerated or caused his coronary artery disease?

Expert backs into a corner

A: That's questionable, because there — in the records there were some notations to the fact that he had chest pain while fighting fires.

Q: So, in fact, there were some signs in the medical records, some clinical indications that his fire fighting caused or accelerated the disease?

MS. T.: Objection.

A: That is not true.

Q: Well, I don't understand your answer, then, Doctor.

A: OK. I said that there are some indications that he had chest pain. The chest pains that he experienced through 1986 were not felt to be due to heart disease because the catheterizations demonstrated insignificant coronary artery disease. He did have a peptic ulcer, he did have other problems that could have precipitated chest pain.

Q: Such as?

A: Well, the peptic ulcer could precipitate chest pain, and indeed that's apparently what was felt in 1974 to have caused his admission. His discharge diagnosis at — in 1974, after that chest pain, did not include coronary artery disease as a cause of his chest pain.

Q: You would agree, though, that coronary artery disease can cause chest pain?

A: Oh, sure.

Q: He had some lung disease too, didn't he?

A: It was questionable. Some of the physicians reported that he had lung disease due to smoking. Dr. Kravitz did some pulmonary function tests and did not find any abnormality. So that — that was in dispute, whether or not he had chronic bronchitis.

Q: OK.

A: In fact, one of the hospitalizations more recently showed that his pulmonary function studies were normal.

Q: And, Doctor, it's — it's your feeling that the progression of the claimant's disease was normal?

A: The progression of the claimant's disease was commensurate with his type for hyperlipidemia and the other risk factors that he demonstrated. I might add that there was a progression of his disease after he retired between 1990 and 1992.

Q: OK. Doctor, I want to go back to what we talked about in the beginning about firefighters and coronary artery disease.

Counsel persists on opinion issue

Q: So that the jury and I are absolutely clear, Doctor, and then I'll stop asking the questions, is it your opinion that the inhalation of smoke, fumes, and toxic gases associated with fire fighting is not a risk factor for developing coronary artery disease?

A: It is not only my opinion, it — there is nowhere in the literature that this is an established risk factor for the development of coronary artery disease, although I personally find in favor of firefighters when there are no other risk factors associated with the development of coronary artery disease. I think that's clear. I can make it no clearer.

Q: Doctor, I'm going to ask the court reporter to read you back the question.

A: OK.

Q: And I'm going to ask if you could answer the question with a yes or a no.

    MS. T.: Objection.

Q: If you can't answer it with a yes or a no, tell me.

A: OK.

Q: But I'm going to ask you to listen closely to the question as the court reporter —

A: OK.

Q: — reads it back and tell me a yes or a no.

    MS. T.: Objection to this.

A: I cannot answer it with a yes or a no other than the way I just answered it.

Counsel persists and finally gets an explanation

Q: OK. And when you say that you find in favor of firefighters, does that mean that you personally — I don't care what the literature says — that you personally have the opinion that the inhalation of smoke, gases and toxic fumes associated with fire fighting can cause coronary artery disease?

Your objection is noted. Go ahead, Doctor.

A: Repeat the question since there had been some dialogue between the question and the answer.

Q: Would you read it back, please?

A: As I mentioned before, I — I still do not know, on a clinical basis, whether this is a fact, however, when there are no other risk factors and a firefighter develops coronary artery disease, that is what I mean by finding in favor of it. I find the relationship to be positive, even though I do not have clinical evidence for it in the literature nor in any clinical experience of anyone that I know of throughout the country.

I mean, if you — if you look at Breunwald or Hurst or the established treatises in cardiology, nowhere is there — is that established as a risk factor for coronary artery disease.

Q: OK. And so we're clear, Doctor, when we talk about risk factors in the realm of coronary artery disease, those are what we mean by causes, because we can't pinpoint a single cause, is that correct?

A: No, that's not correct. Not as cause as we would think of a bacteria causing pneumonia. A relationship is not necessarily a cause. We don't know how the — how it comes about, but there is a relationship between the two. A cause and effect has not been established.

Counsel starts to knock out defenses

Q: OK. So you can't say, to a reasonable degree of medical certainty, whether smoking causes coronary artery disease, correct, Doctor?

A: Causes it?

Q: Causes it.

      MS. T.: Objection.

A: No. It's — it's related to it.

Q: OK. The same thing regarding diabetes. You can't say diabetes causes coronary artery disease?

A: That is correct.

Q: And that would be true of all of the risk factors that you stated. All we can say is those things are in a relationship?

A: That when those —

     MS. T.: Objection.

A: — risk factors are present a person is prone or likely to develop coronary artery disease.

Q: OK. And that's a limitation that's placed on us by what we know, medical science just hasn't got that far?

A: That's exactly right.

Counsel corners expert

Q: OK. Based on what you told me about the connection between inhalation of smoke and fumes and firefighters and your understanding of the medical literature, is there such a thing as firefighters' heart disease?

A: To my knowledge, in a clinical sense, in the medical perspective, there is not an established firefighters' heart disease. In other words, if a pathologist had a heart in his hand and someone asked, "Was this disease caused by fire fighting?," there is not an exact lesion or identifying mark that says this was caused by fire fighting.

Counsel asks key question

Q: OK. Now, Doctor, I'm going to ask you a question. Is it your opinion, Doctor, that a cardiovascular disease of a firefighter can be caused by the cumulative effect of exposure to heat, the inhalation of smoke, toxic gases, chemical fumes, and other toxic substances in the performance of his duty?

A: I recognize that that is a potential, even though I do not have specific clinical evidence to that in the medical literature.

Counsel asks "Is it possible?" question

Q: So, you're saying that it is possible?

     MS. T.: Objection. Asked and answered several times.

A: I said I recognize it as a potential. If you want to interpret that as it is possible, I — I already mentioned to you that I do find in favor of firefighters when there are no other extenuating circumstances.

Q: Doctor, you keep saying you find in favor of firefighters. Are you a judge?

A: No. I — I already mentioned that I do give opinions to the Industrial Commission, and that's what I mean by finding in favor of. If you would like me to —

Q: So, you give opinions to the Industrial Commission that working as a firefighter causes cardiovascular disease?

      MS. T.: Objection.

A: In certain situations I have given that opinion, yes.

Q: In the present case, Doctor, you don't believe that the claimant's work as a firefighter had anything to do with his cardiovascular disease?

A: I think I mentioned that I find no clinical evidence that it — it accelerated or produced his coronary artery disease.

Q: Well, what clinical evidence would you expect to find, Doctor?

A: An individual without any risk factors, without the disease of hyperlipidemia who is a young person and develops heart disease without any other cause who is a firefighter.

Counsel elicits rule-out diagnosis

Q: I see. So, in fact, your opinion as to firefighters and cardiovascular disease is a rule-out diagnosis. If you find no other risk factors, then you'll, as a last chance, fall back on that position?

A: I think that's a fair characterization, that — that generally it is a rule-out diagnosis. If there is other over — if there is — if there are not other overwhelming causes of an individual's heart disease, yes, I would agree with you.

Counsel rephrases expert's reply

Q: OK. So, unless somebody is risk-free and a firefighter, you don't think that fire fighting can cause his disease?

A: I didn't say that. If an individual has family history that is mild or weak, or has well-controlled diabetes, or has a minimal risk factor, that might well be a situation where I would find that there was a relationship between a firefighter and his heart disease. If an individual has six risk factors and the disease of hyperlipidemia No. IV, as in this situation, I would not find.

Q: OK. In an individual with controlled diabetes, and a firefighter, and cardiovascular disease, how do you know, Doctor, that the cardiovascular disease was contracted by work as a firefighter and not the result of the well-controlled diabetes?

A: Well, if you're giving me a hypothetical, that's one thing. If you want me to rule on such a case, you would have to give me the history. We— we rely a lot on historical data.

Q: Let's an — let's pose it as a hypothetical, then, Doctor.

Counsel gets expert to argue

A: Then give me a specific case. Give me the age, how well the diabetes is controlled, how long the individual has been a firefighter, if there's a family history, if the individual has a condition of triglyceride abnormalities.

Q: Are you backing off from your position, then, Doctor, and changing your view about whether cardiovascular disease can be contracted in — during the work as a firefighter?

A: Give me — a specific incident and I'll give you an answer.

Counsel badgers witness

Q: I see. Well, I think you threw the hypothetical back at me, Doctor, as the instance where you may find that there's a causal connection. Remember?

A: I'm well aware of what I said, yes.

Q: OK. Now you'd like me to qualify and give you some more details for your position?

A: We rely upon historical data, as I've done in this case, to come to a conclusion or give an opinion. Give me the historical data of any situation and I'll give you the opinion.

Q: OK. And a history is a very important part of the case, isn't it?

A: Yes, it is.

Q: In fact, it may be the most important part of the case?

Expert inadvertently says history is important and counsel seizes his opportunity

Q: Well, no, not in all — in cardiology, we have objective evidence, fortunately. In this situation, the history was very important, but the cardiac catherizations proved to be even more important.

OK. But you never had an opportunity to take the history directly from the claimant?

A: That is correct.

Q: OK. Now, Doctor, in your report you mentioned that the claimant may have had some other outside employment besides being a firefighter. Did you see some evidence of that in the records that you reviewed?

A: Yes, I did.

Q: And it's your opinion, Doctor, that his outside work had absolutely nothing to do with his development of coronary artery disease?

   MS. T.: Objection.

A: That I had no evidence that his outside work caused his coronary artery disease, I believe that's what I stated.

Q: OK. No evidence that it contributed to his coronary artery disease?

A: Um-hum.

Counsel gets expert to hypothesize

Q: What kind of evidence would you need?

A: I — I'd have to think about that a good while. I'm not sure that I would come up with hypotheticals as far as the evidence that I would need. For instance — I don't — I don't know. I really would have to be given the facts and then I would have to come up with — with a conclusion.

Q: Let's assume that the claimant was under some financial stresses during the 1970s and 1980s. Financial concerns at home.

A: Um-hum.

Q: Would that cause or — his — or accelerate his coronary artery disease?

A: I think I mentioned before — and I — I did read some of that, and I believe it was in the deposition — that there is no specific evidence that chronic stress causes coronary artery disease or accelerates it, and this is under the category of chronic stress, of which we are all exposed.

Q: OK. Let's assume that the claimant worked another job as a trucker.

A: Um-hum.

Q: Would that have any relation in terms of cause or acceleration for his coronary artery disease?

A: To my knowledge, there's no relationship of truck driving to the development of, or aggravation of, coronary artery disease.

Q: Let's assume that the claimant's wife was suffering some emotional problems at home. Would that have any relation via cause or aggravation to his coronary artery disease?

A: I would answer it the same way I did as a truck driver. I have no clinical evidence that that kind of relationship causes or accelerates coronary artery disease.

Counsel obtains admission from expert

Q: OK. Finally, Doctor, your opinion is that the claimant indeed does have coronary artery disease, correct?

A: Yes, it is.

Q: And your opinion is that, despite his age, his condition has progressed normally as you would expect in somebody with his level of disease and risk factors, is that correct?

A: His level of disease, risk factors and disease of hyperlipidemia No. IV, yes.

Q: OK. Now, Doctor, is hyperdemia — hyperlipidemia No. IV a more important risk factor than the fact that he was a smoker?

A: It depends upon the amount of smoking, the length of time.

Q: Well, you know all that stuff —

A: Thirty years at —

Q: — in this case, Doctor.

A: Well, there's a discrepancy of — I believe he said one pack a day and there — and the history, the historical data said two packs a day for thirty years. Two packs a day is quite significant for thirty years.

Counsel uses expert's prior testimony

Q: But, in fact, Doctor, what you told us before remains true, that as a medical scientist you can't tell us whether the hyperlipidemia was any more, or less, of a causative factor than his smoking?

A: That is a fair characterization.

Q: OK. And you don't have any opinion, Doctor, of your own knowledge as to whether inhalation of smoke, fumes, or toxic gases was a causative factor to his heart disease?

Expert appears to tire

A: That is exactly what I said before. If you would like to read it again, fine. I don't recall the — the exact words.

Q: OK. And, Doctor, you don't have any opinion — you can't tell us whether the claimant's diabetes was any more, or less, of a causative factor than anything else in developing his coronary artery disease?

A: Yes, I think that I can state that. We cardiologists believe that smoking cigarettes is an overwhelming risk factor. We also believe that hyperlipidemia is an overwhelming risk factor. The well-controlled diabetic who does not have an elevated cholesterol or triglyceride is not in the same category as a diabetic who has an elevated cholesterol and triglyceride.

Q: OK, Doctor, just a few more questions. In your study of cardiology and, I'm sure, of heart disease I'm sure that you've paid a lot of attention to smoking. Correct?

A: Yes, I'll —

Counsel compares smoking to fire fighting

Q: Some of us may be smokers and some of us may be not, so let's review for a moment smoking, OK? Smoking cigarettes —

A: Um-hum.

Q: — because that's what the claimant smoked, correct?

A: I believe so.

Q: OK. When an individual takes a cigarette, they place a — a roll of tobacco inside of rice paper to their lips, correct?

A: I'm not sure if it's rice paper or some other type of paper, but yes.

Q: OK. And then they place a flame on the end of that roll and they draw air through the roll of tobacco, correct?

A: That is correct.

Q: OK. And, then most smokers then take the— the smoke that's produced by the burning tobacco and breathe it into their lungs, correct?

A: That is correct.

Q: OK. And they breathe it deep in their lungs and then they blow it back out, correct?

A: That's correct.

Q: OK. And that smoke is — is burning material, correct?

A: That is correct.

Q: And it produces fumes?

A: Well, we believe that —

Q: Does it produce fumes —

A: We — regarding the development of coronary artery disease, the significant — we believe the significant side product of it, we believe, is the — the carbon monoxide, the nicotine and other substances that are indigenous to the cigarette. But all of the ingredients that go into causing — cause and effect, we're not sure of.

Q: OK. But, in any case, Doctor, the question was the burning of cigarettes causes fumes, correct?

A: Causes fumes, OK.

177

Q: Yes. OK. And you would agree with me that carbon monoxide that's produced in the burning of the tobacco is a gas?

A: Yes.

Q: And carbon monoxide, in fact, is a toxic gas, isn't it?

A: Yes, it is.

Q: OK. And it's a toxic substance in —

A: Yes.

Q: — the right degree?

A: Yes, it is.

Q: OK. So cigarette smokers breathe in fumes, gases and toxic substances into their lungs and exhale them, correct?

A: Yes.

Counsel leads expert to conclusion

Q: OK. And medical science, in at least studying smoking, has determined that this action precipitates or at least is a significant risk factor in the development of coronary artery disease, correct?

A: That this action is related to coronary artery disease as a risk factor, correct.

Q: OK. And, so, when you get smokers, you say, "Well, don't smoke, because you don't want to inhale this — this stuff," right?

A: That is correct.

Q: OK. And it's true, Doctor, that people that smoke pipes, for example, that don't inhale develop different kinds of cancers but not the same —

A: They —

Q: — coronary artery disease as cigarette smokers, who take the smoke into their lungs, correct?

A: That appears to be so.

Q: OK. Doctor, in all of the records you reviewed, what kind of evidence did you see about respiratory protection provided to the claimant while he was fighting fires?

A: I didn't come across any.

Q: Do you know if he was provided with respiratory protection?

A: I do not know that.

Q: Thanks, Doctor. Nothing further.

Recross-Examination

By Mr. S.:

Counsel shows doctor was not thorough

> **Q:** Doctor, how do you know if the materials before you constitute the complete record of the medical records of the claimant?
>
> **A:** I do not know that for a fact.
>
> **Q:** If you met with the claimant, you could have asked him where he was hospitalized, couldn't you?
>
> **A:** Yes.
>
> **Q:** You could have asked him if he was seen by any other doctors?
>
> **A:** Yes.
>
> **Q:** You could have asked about other studies?
>
> **A:** Yes.
>
> **Q:** So, Doctor, the opinion that you stated here today and the records that you've relied upon in preparing this opinion have come solely from the attorney, Mr. J., correct?
>
> **A:** The — the records that I relied upon —
>
> The records that I relied upon have come solely from Mr. J.
>
> **Q:** OK. Thanks, Doctor. Nothing further.

Conclusion

Expert witnesses have the daunting task of investigation, analysis, reaching an opinion, and testifying to that opinion under the pains and penalties of perjury in an open courtroom. One of the most challenging aspects of being an expert witness is the rigors of cross-examination. The authors trust that reviewing this text will help remove much of the anxiety caused by cross-examination and will help you excel during cross-examination.

Appendix A Cross-Examination Checklist

__ Understand the issues.

__ Curriculum vitae is 100% accurate.

__ Know what your retaining attorney needs to prove or disprove.

__ Have all the relevant facts.

__ Organize your documents.

__ Dress appropriately.

__ Have a reasonable basis to discount the opposing expert's opinion.

__ Use accepted methodology.

__ Appear unbiased.

__ Do not become argumentative.

__ Maintain composure and do not seem arrogant.

__ Offer no opinions which defy common sense.

__ Listen carefully to questions.

__ Pause before giving responses.

__ Do not volunteer information.

__ Be at ease.

__ Prepare thoroughly.

__ Refer to exhibits by number.

__ Refer to notes at appropriate times.

__ Be an expert, not an advocate.

__ Talk to the jury — not to the attorney or judge.

__ Do not condescend to the jury.

__ Do not use slang.

__ If you need a break, ask for one.

__ If questioned about a document, ask to see it.

__ If interrupted, finish your answer.

Appendix B Trick and Difficult Questions

How many times have you testified in the last five years?

How many times have you testified on behalf of plaintiffs?

How many times have you testified on behalf of defendants?

What percentage of your income in 1995 was generated as a result of being a litigation consultant and expert witness?

How much are you being paid for your testimony here today?

Please list the articles you have published on _____.

Is _____ a recognized expert in this field?

What are the authoritative textbooks in this area?

How else do you advertise that, for a price, you are available to testify?

What documents did you review before forming your opinion?

On what factual assumptions is your opinion based?

How many times have you spoken to or met with Attorney Jones regarding your work on this case?

When did you first form your opinion?

Have you ever given an erroneous opinion?

Please describe the financial interest you have in the defendant corporation.

Who first contacted you regarding this case?

What was the methodology that you followed to arrive at your opinion?

Is your methodology accepted in your field?

If the assumptions on which your opinion is based were to change, could that change your opinion?

You don't have any practical experience in this particular subspecialty, do you?

Isn't it a fact that you have had no special training or experience in the precise discipline on which you have given your opinion?

You didn't witness the events in question, did you?

What is your fee to date for work on this case?

How many times in the past five years have you been retained by the plaintiff?

How many times in the past five years have you been retained by Attorney Jones or his law firm?

What is your understanding of the term "reasonable degree of scientific certainty"?

Do you still have a substance abuse problem?

In forming your opinion did you review _____?

If you were to assume if _____ were true, would that change your opinion?

You've never received a research or teaching fellowship, have you?

"Yes" or "no," please answer the question.

Is there anything that you don't consider yourself an expert on?

Didn't you give a contrary opinion during your testimony in the *Jones* case in 1991?

Didn't you embrace the other view in the article you had published dated June 22, 1991?

Well, Doctor, following your reasoning, wouldn't a _____ result occur?

Isn't it a fact that your brother is a partner in Mr. Jones' law firm?

Isn't it a fact that your daughter works for the defendant corporation?

Is this a copy of the ad you had placed in _____?

What other expert witness referral services do you pay to be listed with?

You have no way of verifying the facts provided to you by Attorney Smith, do you?

What is the biggest weakness in your opinion?

What did attorney Jones tell you in your eleven meetings and conversations with him?

You disagree with all the recognized experts in this field, don't you?

Could it be that you are just plain wrong?

Appendix C Rules of Civil Procedure and Evidence

All expert witnesses should familiarize themselves with the Federal Rules of Civil Procedure and Evidence that apply to their testimony. While you will not be arguing points of law with the attorneys, it is helpful to understand the rules that control the litigation. Note that because your state and local rules may vary from the federal rules, you should obtain and compare them with the federal rules abstracted below.

Federal Rules of Civil Procedure

Rule 26. General Provisions Governing Discovery; Duty of Disclosure

Disclosure of Expert Testimony.

(A) In addition to the disclosures required by paragraph (1), a party shall disclose to other parties the identity of any person who may be used at trial to present evidence under Rules 702, 703, or 705 of the Federal Rules of Evidence.

(B) Except as otherwise stipulated or directed by the court, this disclosure shall, with respect to a witness who is retained or specially employed to provide expert testimony in the case or whose duties as an employee of the party regularly involve giving expert testimony, be accompanied by a written report prepared and signed by the witness. The report shall contain a complete statement of all opinions to be expressed and the basis and reasons therefor; the data or other information considered by the witness in forming the opinions; any exhibits to be used as a summary of or support for the opinions; the qualifications of the witness, including a list of all publications authored by the witness within the preceding ten years; the compensation to be paid for the study and testimony; and a listing of any other cases in which the witness has testified as an expert at trial or by deposition within the preceding four years.

(C) These disclosures shall be made at the times and in the sequence directed by the court. In the absence of other directions from the court or stipulation by the parties, the disclosures shall be made at least 90 days before the trial date or the date the case is to be ready for trial or, if the evidence is intended solely to contradict or rebut evidence on the same subject matter identified by another party under paragraph (2)(B), within 30 days after the disclosure made by the other party. The parties shall supplement these disclosures when required under subdivision (e)(1).

The advisory committee notes provide an explanation and interpretation of Rule 26(2)(B) as follows:

Paragraph (2)(B) requires that persons retained or specially employed to provide expert testimony, or whose duties as an employee of the party regularly involve the giving of expert testimony, must prepare a detailed and complete written report, stating the testimony the witness is expected to present during direct examination, together with the reasons therefor. The information disclosed under the former rule in answering interrogatories about the "substance" of expert testimony was frequently so sketchy and vague that it rarely dispensed with the need to depose the expert and often was even of little help in preparing for a deposition of the witness. Revised Rule 37(c)(1) provides an incentive for full disclosure; namely, that a party will not ordinarily be permitted to use on direct examination any expert testimony not so disclosed. Rule 26(a)(2)(B) does not preclude counsel from providing assistance to experts in preparing the reports, and indeed, with experts such as automobile mechanics, this assistance may be needed. Nevertheless, the report, which is intended to set forth the substance of the direct examination, should be written in a manner that reflects the testimony to be given by the witness and it must be signed by the witness.

The report is to disclose the data and other information considered by the expert and any exhibits or charts that summarize or support the expert's opinions. Given this obligation of disclosure, litigants should no longer be able to argue that materials furnished to their experts to be used in forming their opinions — whether or not ultimately relied upon by the expert — are privileged or otherwise protected from disclosure when such persons are testifying or being deposed.

Revised subdivision (b)(4)(A) authorizes the deposition of expert witnesses. Since depositions of experts required to prepare a written report may be taken only after the report has been served, the length of the deposition of such experts should be reduced, and in many cases the report may eliminate the need for a deposition. Revised subdivision (e)(1) requires disclosure of any material changes made in the opinions of an expert from whom a report is required, whether the changes are in the written report or in testimony given at a deposition.

(4) Trial Preparation: Experts.

(A) A party may depose any person who has been identified as an expert whose opinions may be presented at trial. If a report from the expert is required under subdivision (a)(2)(B), the deposition shall not be conducted until after the report is provided.

(B) A party may, through interrogatories or by deposition, discover facts known or opinions held by an expert who has been retained or specially employed by another party in anticipation of litigation or preparation for trial and who is not expected to be called as a witness at trial, only as provided in Rule 35(b) or upon a showing of exceptional circumstances under which it is impracticable for the party seeking discovery to obtain facts or opinions on the same subject by other means:

(C) Unless manifest injustice would result, (I) the court shall require that the party seeking discovery pay the expert a reasonable fee for time spent in responding to discovery under this subdivision; and (ii) with respect to discovery obtained under subdivision (b)(4)(B) of this rule the court shall require the party seeking discovery to pay the other party a fair portion of the fees and expenses reasonable incurred by the latter party in obtaining facts and opinions from the expert.

Federal Rules of Evidence

Rule 601. General Rule of Competency

Every person is competent to be a witness except as otherwise provided in these rules. However, in civil actions and proceedings, with respect to an element of a claim or defense as to which State law supplies the rule of decision, the competency of a witness shall be determined in accordance with State law.

Rule 602. Lack of Personal Knowledge

A witness may not testify to a matter unless evidence is introduced sufficient to support a finding that the witness has personal knowledge of the matter. Evidence to prove personal knowledge may, but need not, consist of the witness' own testimony. This rule is subject to the provisions of rule 703, relating to opinion testimony by the expert witnesses.

Rule 607. Who May Impeach

The credibility of a witness may be attacked by any party, including the party calling the witness.

Rule 608. Evidence of Character and Conduct of Witness

(a) Opinion and reputation evidence of character. The credibility of a witness may be attacked or supported by evidence in the form of opinion or reputation, but subject to these limitations: (1) the evidence may refer only to character for truthfulness or untruthfulness, and (2) evidence of truthful character is admissible only after the character of the witness for truthfulness has been attacked by opinion or reputation evidence or otherwise.

(b) Specific instances of conduct. Specific instances of the conduct of a witness, for the purpose of attacking or supporting the witness' credibility, other than conviction of crime as provided in rule 609, may not be proved by extrinsic evidence. They may, however, in the discretion of the court, if probative of truthfulness or untruthfulness, be inquired into on cross-examination of the witness (1) concerning the witness' character for truthfulness or untruthfulness, or (2) concerning the character for truthfulness or untruthfulness of another witness as to which character the witness being cross-examined has testified.

The giving of testimony, whether by an accused or by any other witness, does not operate as a waiver of the accused's or the witness' privilege against self-incrimination when examined with respect to matters which relate only to credibility.

Rule 609. Impeachment by Evidence of Conviction of Crime

(a) General rule. For the purpose of attacking the credibility of a witness,

(1) evidence that a witness other than an accused has been convicted of a crime shall be admitted, subject to Rule 403, if the crime was punishable by death or imprisonment in excess of one year under the law under which the witness was convicted, and evidence that an accused has been convicted of such a crime shall be admitted if the court determines that the probative value of admitting this evidence outweighs its prejudicial effect to the accused; and

(2) evidence that any witness has been convicted of a crime shall be admitted if it involved dishonesty or false statement, regardless of the punishment.

(b) Time limit. Evidence of a conviction under this rule is not admissible if a period of more than ten years has elapsed since the date of the conviction or of the release of the witness from the confinement imposed for that conviction, whichever is the later date, unless the court determines, in the interests of justice, that the probative value of the conviction supported by specific facts and circumstances substantially outweighs its prejudicial effect. However, evidence of a conviction more than 10 years old as calculated herein, is not admissible unless the proponent gives to the adverse party sufficient advance written notice of intent to use such evidence to provide the adverse party with a fair opportunity to contest the use of such evidence.

(c) Effect of pardon, annulment, or certificate of rehabilitation. Evidence of a conviction is not admissible under this rule if (1) the conviction has been the subject of a pardon, annulment, certificate of rehabilitation, or other equivalent procedure based on a finding of the rehabilitation of the person convicted, and that person has not been convicted of a subsequent crime which was punishable by death or imprisonment in excess of one year, or (2) the conviction has been the subject of a pardon, annulment, or other equivalent procedure based on a finding of innocence.

(d) Juvenile adjudications. Evidence of juvenile adjudications is generally not admissible under this rule. The court may, however, in a criminal case allow evidence of a juvenile adjudication of a witness other than the accused if conviction of the offense would be admissible to attack the credibility of an adult and the court is satisfied that admission in evidence is necessary for a fair determination of the issue of guilt or innocence.

(e) Pendency of appeal. The pendency of an appeal therefrom does not render evidence of a conviction inadmissible. Evidence of the pendency of an appeal is admissible.

Rule 611. Mode and Order of Interrogation and Presentation

(a) Control by court. The court shall exercise reasonable control over the mode and order of interrogating witnesses and presenting evidence so as to (1) make the interrogation and presentation effective for the ascertainment of the truth, (2) avoid needless consumption of time, and (3) protect witnesses from harassment or undue embarrassment.

(b) Scope of cross-examination. Cross-examination should be limited to the subject matter of the direct examination and matters affecting the credibility of the witness. The court may, in the exercise of discretion, permit inquiry into additional matters as if on direct examination.

(c) Leading questions. Leading questions should not be used on the direct examination of a witness except as may be necessary to develop the witness' testimony. Ordinarily leading questions should be permitted on cross-examination. When a party calls a hostile witness, an adverse party, or a witness identified with an adverse party, interrogation may be by leading question.

Rule 613. Prior Statements of Witnesses

(a) Examining witness concerning prior statement. In examining a witness concerning a prior statement made by the witness, whether written or not, the statement need not be shown nor its contents disclosed to the witness at that time, but on request the same shall be shown or disclosed to opposing counsel.

(b) Extrinsic evidence of prior inconsistent statement of witness. Extrinsic evidence of a prior inconsistent statement by a witness is not admissible unless the witness is afforded an opportunity to explain or deny the same and the opposite party is afforded an opportunity to interrogate the witness thereon, or the interests of justice otherwise require. This provision does not apply to admissions of a party-opponent as defined in rule 801(d)(2).

Rule 701. Opinion Testimony by Lay Witnesses

If the witness is not testifying as an expert, the witness' testimony in the form of opinions or inferences is limited to those opinions or inferences which are (a) rationally based on the perception of the witness and (b) helpful to a clear understanding of the witness' testimony or the determination of a fact in issue.

Rule 702. Testimony by Experts

If scientific, technical, or other specialized knowledge will assist the trier of fact to understand the evidence or to determine a fact in issue, a witness qualified as an expert by knowledge, skill, experience, training, or education, may testify thereto in the form of an opinion or otherwise.

Rule 703. Bases of Opinion Testimony by Experts

The facts or data in the particular case upon which an expert bases an opinion may be those perceived by or made known to the expert at or before the hearing. If of a type reasonably relied upon by experts in the particular field in forming opinions or inferences upon the subject, the facts or data need not be admissible in evidence.

Rule 704. Opinion on Ultimate Issue

(a) Except as provided in subdivision (b), testimony in the form of an opinion or inference otherwise admissible is not objectionable because it embraces an ultimate issue to be decided by the trier of fact.

(b) No expert witness testifying with respect to the mental state or condition of a defendant in a criminal case may state an opinion or inference as to whether the defendant did or did not have the mental state or condition constituting an element of the crime charged or of a defense thereto. Such ultimate issues are matters for the trier of fact alone.

Rule 705. Disclosure of Facts or Data Underlying Expert Opinion

The expert may testify in terms of opinion or inference and give reasons therefor without first testifying to the underlying facts or data, unless the court requires otherwise. The expert may in any event be required to disclose the underlying facts or data on cross-examination.

Rule 706. Court Appointed Experts

(a) Appointment. The court may on its own motion or on the motion of any party enter an order to show cause why expert witnesses should not be appointed, and may request the parties to submit nominations. The court may appoint any expert witnesses agreed upon by the parties, and may appoint expert witnesses of its own selection. An expert witness shall not be appointed by the court unless the witness consents to act. A witness so appointed shall be informed of the witness' duties by the court in writing, a copy of which shall be filed with the clerk, or at a conference in which the parties shall have opportunity to participate. A witness so appointed shall advise the parties of the witness' findings, if any; the witness' deposition may be taken by any party; and the witness may be called to testify by the court or any party. The witness shall be subject to cross-examination by each party, including a party calling the witness.

(b) Compensation. Expert witnesses so appointed are entitled to reasonable compensation in whatever sum the court may allow. The compensation thus fixed is payable from funds which may be provided by law in criminal cases and civil actions and proceedings involving just compensation under the fifth amendment. In other civil actions and proceedings the compensation shall be paid by the parties in such proportion and at such time as the court directs, and thereafter charged in like manner as other costs.

(c) Disclosure of appointment. In the exercise of its discretion, the court may authorize disclosure to the jury of the fact that the court appointed the expert witness.

(d) Parties' experts of own selection. Nothing in this rule limits the parties in calling expert witnesses of their own selection.

Rule 1005. Public Records

The contents of an official record, or of a document authorized to be recorded or filed and actually recorded or filed, including data compilations in any form, if otherwise admissible, may be proved by copy, certified as correct in accordance with rule 902 or testified to be correct by a witness who has compared it with the original. If a copy which complies with the foregoing cannot be obtained by the exercise of reasonable diligence, then other evidence of the contents may be given.

Rule 1006. Summaries

The contents of voluminous writings, recordings, or photographs which cannot conveniently be examined in court may be presented in the form of a chart, summary, or calculation. The originals, or duplicates, shall be made available for examination or copying, or both, by other parties at reasonable time and place. The court may order that they be produced in court.

Rule 1007. Testimony or Written Admission of Party

Contents of writings, recordings, or photographs may be proved by the testimony or deposition of the party against whom offered or by that party's written admission, without accounting for the nonproduction of the original.

Appendix D Evidentiary Flow Chart

The flow chart presented on the following two pages explains Federal Rules of Evidence 701-704. This graphical explanation was prepared by Professor David L. Faigman, who is a professor of law at the University of California, Hastings College of the Law.

Opinion, Expert Testimony
[Rules: 701; 702; 703; 704]
Opinion testimony by lay witnesses;
Testimony by experts;
Bases of opinion testimony by experts;
Opinion on ultimate issue.

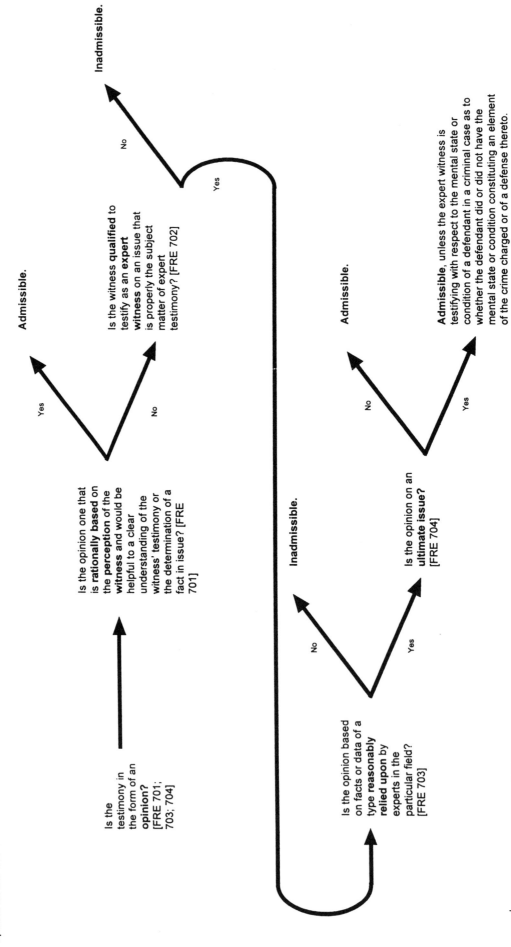

Is the testimony in the form of an opinion? [FRE 701; 703; 704]

Is the opinion one that is **rationally based** on the **perception** of the witness and would be helpful to a clear understanding of the witness' testimony or the determination of a fact in issue? [FRE 701]

Yes → **Admissible.**

No → Is the witness qualified to testify as an **expert witness** on an issue that is properly the subject matter of expert testimony? [FRE 702]

No → **Inadmissible.**

Yes →

Is the opinion based on facts or data of a type reasonably **relied upon** by experts in the particular field? [FRE 703]

No → **Inadmissible.**

Yes → Is the opinion on an **ultimate issue?** [FRE 704]

No → **Admissible.**

Yes → **Admissible,** unless the expert witness is testifying with respect to the mental state or condition of a defendant in a criminal case as to whether the defendant did or did not have the mental state or condition constituting an element of the crime charged or of a defense thereto. [FRE 704]

Expert Testimony
[Rules: 702; 104(a)]
Testimony by experts.

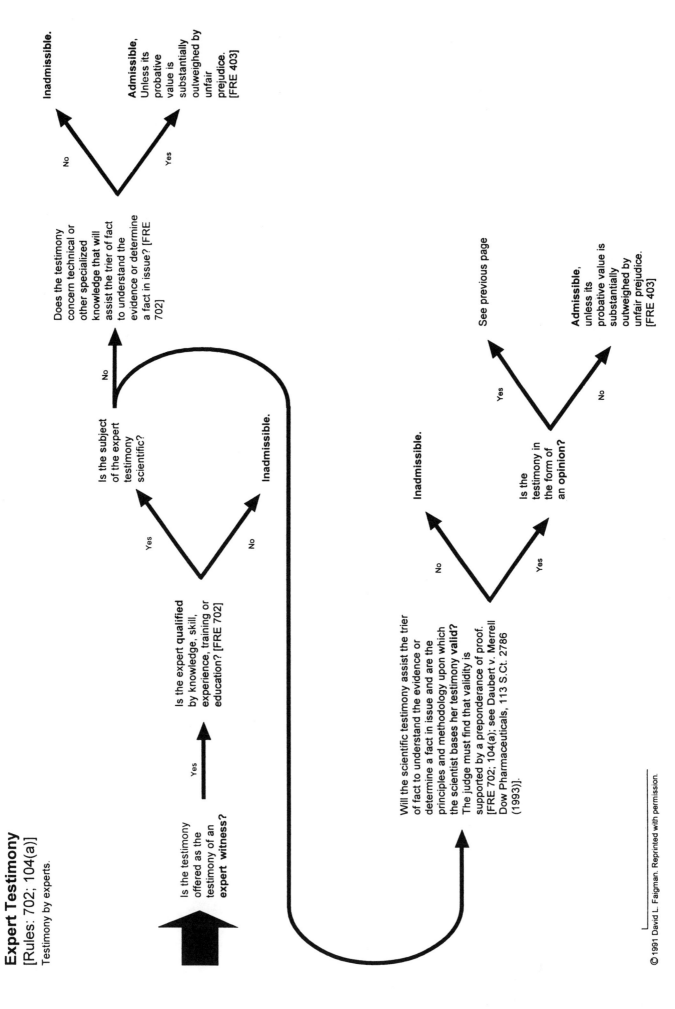

Is the testimony offered as the testimony of an **expert witness?**

Yes →

Is the expert **qualified** by knowledge, skill, experience, training or education? [FRE 702]

Yes → Is the subject of the expert testimony scientific?

No → **Inadmissible.**

No → Does the testimony concern technical or other specialized knowledge that will assist the trier of fact to understand the evidence or determine a fact in issue? [FRE 702]

No → **Inadmissible.**

Yes → **Admissible,** Unless its probative value is substantially outweighed by unfair prejudice. [FRE 403]

Will the scientific testimony assist the trier of fact to understand the evidence or determine a fact in issue and are the principles and methodology upon which the scientist bases her testimony **valid?** The judge must find that validity is supported by a preponderance of proof. [FRE 702; 104(a); see Daubert v. Merrell Dow Pharmaceuticals, 113 S.Ct. 2786 (1993)].

No → **Inadmissible.**

Yes → Is the testimony in the form of an **opinion?**

Yes → See previous page

No → **Admissible,** unless its probative value is substantially outweighed by unfair prejudice. [FRE 403]